RAND

The British Nuclear Deterrent After the Cold War

Nicholas K. J. Witney

Project AIR FORCE

The research reported here was sponsored by the United States Air Force under Contract F49620-91-C-0003. Further information may be obtained from the Strategic Planning Division, Directorate of Plans, Hq USAF.

Library of Congress Cataloging in Publication Data

Witney, Nicholas K. J.
    The British nuclear deterrent after the cold war / Nicholas
K.J. Witney.
        p.   cm
    "Prepared for the United States Air Force."
    "MR-514-AF."
    Includes bibliographical references.
    ISBN 0-8330-1619-9
    1. Nuclear weapons—Great Britain.   2. Deterrence
(Strategy).   3. Great Britain—Military policy.   4. Europe—
Politics and government—1989–   I. United States.   Air Force.
II. Title.
U264.5.G7W58   1995
355.02´17´0941—dc20   94-44369
                                                                                          CIP

RAND is a nonprofit institution that helps improve public policy through research and analysis. RAND's publications do not necessarily reflect the opinions or policies of its research sponsors.

Published 1995 by RAND
1700 Main Street, P.O. Box 2138, Santa Monica, CA 90407-2138
RAND URL: http://www.rand.org/
To order RAND documents or to obtain additional information, contact Distribution
Services: Telephone: (310) 451-7002; Fax: (310) 451-6915; Internet: order@rand.org

RAND

The British Nuclear Deterrent After the Cold War

Nicholas K. J. Witney

Prepared for the
United States Air Force

Project AIR FORCE

PREFACE

This report is a product of work undertaken by the author, a British civil servant, during a year's secondment to RAND from the United Kingdom Ministry of Defence. The views expressed are, however, personal and should not be held to represent those of either organization. The study may be of interest to those who follow British defense issues and wider questions concerning the role of nuclear forces in the post-Cold War era, the problems of proliferation, and the future development of Euro-Atlantic security structures and relations.

The research has been conducted under the Strategy, Doctrine, and Force Structure program of Project AIR FORCE at RAND. Comments and criticisms are invited and should be addressed either to the author or to the program director, Zalmay Khalilzad.

CONTENTS

SUMMARY

The Trident nuclear deterrent program is one of the United Kingdom's largest-ever military acquisitions. Planned and initiated in the depths of the Cold War, it is now coming to fruition, when the most obvious justification for it--the Soviet threat to Western Europe--has disappeared. The continuation of the program is not in doubt; the money is largely spent or committed, and the main political parties agree on deploying the force. But the rationale needs refurbishment.

THE NEED FOR A REDEFINED RATIONALE

Britain has traditionally preferred to represent her nuclear capability primarily as a contribution to NATO's collective deterrence. The "second center of decisionmaking" concept defined a particular value for that contribution. This rationale seized the moral high ground (by associating Britain's deterrent with NATO's strategy to prevent war), guarded the proliferation flank, and underpinned Anglo-American relations.

But the evaporation of the immediate and seemingly overwhelming threat from the East has diminished the plausibility of a rationale based on the assumption of a credibility gap in the U.S. nuclear guarantee to Europe. The British government seems to be moving toward a more generalized rationale based on preservation of the status quo and on insurance against new risks rather than deterrence of old threats. Nevertheless, a specific niche for the U.K. deterrent is harder to discern under this approach, and the shift is made no easier by the reopening of an historic divide between Europe and America in fundamental attitudes toward nuclear weapons.

Different histories and geographical circumstances have disposed Europeans and Americans to different attitudes toward nuclear weapons-- the former being more conscious of their role in preserving peace in Europe and the latter, of their potential for visiting destruction on America. The history of the development of NATO's strategy, including Flexible Response and the Strategic Concept of 1991, is that of the management and synthesis of these different attitudes. But the end of the Cold War, the success of U.S. conventional arms in the Gulf War, and the quickened awareness of the dangers of nuclear proliferation have combined to reopen the divide. A new administration has come to power in a U.S. intellectual climate now widely disposed to question the utility, even the legitimacy, of nuclear power in international affairs.

The main policy thrusts to which this attitudinal shift gives rise--denuclearization and counterproliferation--pose no problems for the United Kingdom. But there is potential for friction, starting at the conceptual level, over the reflexive elements of America's altered approach to nuclear issues. Traditional NATO doctrine has cast nuclear weapons (in the right hands and circumstances) as net assets to international security--as "Blessings in Disguise." This is clearly a position that the present British government seeks to preserve (reinterpreted as necessary) for the U.K. nuclear deterrent. The new U.S. intellectual climate, however, suggests a wholly different characterization of nuclear power--that of an "Ultimate Evil"--a capability which, if it cannot be abolished, should at least be marginalized.

Divergence between Washington and London on the role of nuclear weapons in international security seems unlikely to jeopardize the historically close bilateral nuclear cooperation of the two nations, at least at the technical level. Both sides continue to benefit significantly by it. The U.K. gets the "leverage" effect of being able to maintain an operationally independent nuclear capability at a fraction of the costs incurred by France. The United States benefits both economically and strategically. But the perception by both parties of national advantage in continuing technical cooperation does not guarantee that the special intimacy of past relations in the field of broader nuclear policy will endure. On the contrary, the "de-emphasizing" of nuclear weapons must inevitably reduce the nuclear-cooperation element of Anglo-American relations and increase the risk of diverging attitudes.

Recent transatlantic friction over nuclear testing illustrates how diverging attitudes could cause the political charge of U.S.-U.K.

interaction on nuclear issues to change from positive to neutral, or even to negative--further weakening an already diminished bilateral relationship. If this risk is to be avoided, and if transatlantic nuclear cooperation is to continue on the same basis of mutual confidence and benefit as in the past, then it will be important for Britain to reformulate the rationale for its deterrent in terms that enable Americans to continue to regard it as a net asset to international security, despite the transformation of the international environment with the end of the Cold War. The problem is approached by examining in turn three candidate "alternative" rationales for the U.K. deterrent in the post-Cold War world.

OPTION ONE: A "CATALYST FOR DENUCLEARIZATION"?

One option would be, in conformity with the new U.S. mood, to re-cast the U.K. nuclear deterrent into the role of a "catalyst for denuclearization." Such a concept would value the U.K. nuclear capability less as a deterrent than as a source of moral and political capital with which to purchase international progress on disarmament and nonproliferation. Major reductions in the U.K. capability have already been announced; even when Trident is fully in service, the level of the U.K. nuclear arsenal, measured in megatonnage, will be 25 percent down at the end of the Cold War. But the catalyst approach would aim to take this further, with the conscious and primary purpose of promoting denuclearization elsewhere.

This approach, animated by the Ultimate Evil view of nuclear weapons, would conflict with and tend to undermine the current NATO consensus on nuclear matters. In the past, such a prospect would have implied unacceptable damage to Alliance cohesion. The old nuclear policies and the practical and institutional arrangements associated with them have historically constituted much of NATO's internal glue. But, with or without conscious policy change, such arrangements now have an air of obsolescence about them; and the Alliance will need to find new roles if it is to retain cohesion and viability for the future. Nor does the position of the United States as *primus inter pares*, important though this may remain for Alliance stability, require preservation of the nuclear status quo. Continuation of nuclear "business as usual" is neither a necessary nor a sufficient condition for the survival of the Alliance.

However, if considerations of internal cohesion can be largely discounted, fundamental considerations of external security may still argue for retaining NATO's established nuclear policy. Uncertainties over the ultimate direction of developments in the former Soviet Union, and a prudent concern to ensure against the unforeseen, suggest that catalyzing a reaction of nuclear policy change in the Western Alliance would be a risk worth taking only if clear gains could be anticipated in terms of disarmament or nonproliferation.

On the other hand, it might be hard to construct the linkages that would allow U.K. nuclear reductions to be traded for worthwhile cutbacks elsewhere. Under certain radical options to reduce U.S. and Russian strategic arsenals to minimal levels, the readiness of other nuclear-weapon states to make proportionate cuts might be welcome or essential. But on more probable scenarios, further progress on arms control between the nuclear superpowers would likely be hindered rather than helped by the involvement of third parties in a heretofore bilateral process. Nor is the thesis persuasive that repudiation of nuclear force by its Western possessors would influence proliferators to change their minds. Indeed, such a policy change could be counterproductive. It could risk providing a perverse incentive to proliferation amongst friends who have hitherto been content to rely on "extended deterrence," for their security, as well as among potential adversaries who believe they have more to gain by proliferating if the major powers eschew nuclear force. A "catalyst for denuclearization" rationale for the U.K. deterrent thus seems unattractive.

OPTION TWO: A DETERRENT OF NEW THREATS?

A second possible rationale would stress the potential of U.K. nuclear weapons to deter new threats, particularly those arising from the proliferation of weapons of mass destruction (WMD). But the British government is evidently reluctant to make such claims. In part, this may reflect a view that to broadcast the relevance of nuclear deterrence outside the traditional East-West context would sit ill with the advocacy of nonproliferation. Also, genuine uncertainty exists about the effectiveness of *any* nuclear deterrent threat in new contexts and about the "value added" in such circumstances of a specifically British deterrent.

There seems no sufficient case for doubting that those with whom the Western democracies might find themselves in conflict at some future point understand basic deterrent logic. But, absent a developed mutual understanding of the limits of tolerable behavior, the operation of nuclear deterrence will be fraught with greater risks. Moreover, a nuclear threat by a Western democracy will be credible only if the interests involved are so vital as to make resort to nuclear use seem justified; effective deterrence requires some perceived proportionality between interest at stake and damage threatened. Without the old East-West confrontation, establishing this proportionality may problematic. Unless the adversary has first introduced nuclear weapons (or other weapons of mass destruction) into the confrontation, the stakes on his side are likely to be higher (and both sides will be aware of this asymmetry of interest). At the same time, the posing of a credibly circumscribed retaliatory nuclear threat (even one directed not at populations but at power bases) will be all the harder when the root of aggression is perceived to be a regime rather than a monolithic society. Thus, outside the East-West confrontation, the likely paucity of cases in which truly vital Western interests are at stake, and the difficulty of threatening nuclear damage that would not be self-evidently morally and politically intolerable, suggest that deterrence may be more effective in constraining the manner in which conflicts are conducted (that is, in deterring nuclear and perhaps other WMD use by the adversary) than at preventing their occurrence in the first place.

Within that circumscribed role, can any requirement for a specifically British deterrent be identified? The chances of the United Kingdom finding itself involved in mortal confrontation outside Europe, unless in a U.S.-led coalition, seem remote. Nor could Britain reassert the old "second center" thesis in relation to such coalition action, given the inability of any foreseeable adversary to threaten the U.S.

with strategic retaliation. Nonetheless, the British capability might still provide moral and political support for U.S. deterrent power--the role of the posse member to the U.S.'s sheriff. But this modest role would scarcely seem to equate to a new primary rationale for the U.K. deterrent, even if conditions were not politically inopportune to assert it.

OPTION THREE: A "EURODETERRENT"?

The third possible rationale would be to claim for the U.K. deterrent a "European vocation" as an underpinning of the common European defense that the European Union may one day entail. France, which has been undergoing its own crisis of nuclear identity, has promoted such a concept. The British government has made clear its lack of interest in any project tending to the exclusion of the United States from European security. But it also is attracted to the proposition, both as a rationale that might be developed over time to the advantage of Britain's position in Europe and as a hedge against any future diminution of U.S. commitment. It will also have been encouraged by the readiness of a U.S. administration that favors European integration to accept the development of a European security and defense identity as not detrimental to NATO.

Britain has therefore advocated a gradualist approach, encouraging France to consider the implications of extending deterrence over non-nuclear partners and allies and urging closer bilateral cooperation as a means of strengthening the European contribution to collective Alliance deterrence. Significant progress has been made on coordinating nuclear policy and doctrine. The requirement now is to find ways to extend cooperation into technical and operational areas. The need to find satisfactory alternatives to nuclear testing may promote such cooperation, while coordination of nuclear target planning could underline the potential for joint action by the European nuclear powers, without prejudice to the independence or the preexistent commitments of either.

However, the development of a distinctive European nuclear identity for the British and French deterrents would also depend upon the support of nonnuclear European partners, which is currently little in evidence. NATO's "risk- and burden-sharing" arrangements have served to give non-nuclear allies the necessary "ownership" stake in the Alliance's nuclear policy; but it is not obvious how a similar effect could be achieved in a European context. Indeed, the current interest of nonnuclear Europeans might be as much in constraining as in sharing British and French nuclear capabilities. The development of a nuclear dimension for the European Union's "common defense" can therefore be expected, if at all, only at some later stage of European integration. A "European" rationale for the U.K. deterrent cannot be authoritatively claimed for the present, though it may be presaged for the future.

A SYNTHESIS

Thus, none of the three alternative rationales considered is wholly satisfying in itself. The analysis suggests that the most coherent and persuasive the line of argument is one that combines preserving the established Euro-Atlantic security structures with an affirmation of the scope for and desirability of a strengthened European contribution.

It might be tempting to make some concession to the new U.S. climate of opinion by complementing this view of nuclear deterrence in Europe (and the British contribution to it) as a Blessing in Disguise with the adoption of an "Ultimate Evil elsewhere" approach. But this temptation should be resisted. First, such a concession might negatively affect the 1995 Nuclear Non-Proliferation Treaty (NPT) conference, in that the recognized nuclear-weapon states would feel they had "paid" excessively for NPT extension while proliferators went unconstrained. It could also provide gratuitous encouragement to proliferators, especially if assurances of nonuse were strengthened, any new assurances should exclude adversaries armed with chemical and biological, as well as nuclear, weapons. Furthermore, support for deterrence in the European context would be made no easier by excessive deprecation of Western nuclear power elsewhere. For now, agnosticism about the present and future relevance of Western nuclear deterrence in new contexts seems justified and politic.

The end of the Cold War has diminished the force of both the Blessing in Disguise and the Ultimate Evil conceptions of nuclear weapons. If the U.K. nuclear deterrent is to continue to be presented as a net asset to international security, in a manner both intellectually coherent and acceptable to U.S. opinion, then it must continue to be seen as grounded primarily in European security. It can be seen as a contribution to Western insurance against the risks of Russian recidivism; against unforeseen threats materializing from unexpected quarters or in new forms; and against the reemergence of any conception of war between major nation-states as a sensible policy option. Such a rationale may suffice into the twenty-first century; the more distant future should perhaps be left to take care of itself.

ACKNOWLEDGMENTS

This report is a product of a year spent on secondment from the United Kingdom Ministry of Defence to RAND: I am grateful to the former for releasing me and to the latter for making me welcome. My particular thanks are due to Chris Bowie, for help and guidance throughout the year and for undertaking one review of the final draft. I am grateful to Lawrence Freedman for the other review. Among many RAND colleagues who helped me develop my thinking on these issues, Bob Levine and Dean Wilkening, deserve special mention. From outside RAND, I received help, stimulation, and encouragement variously received from David Yost, Olivier Debouzy, Albert Wohlstetter, Sir Michael Quinlan, and Jon Thatcher. Of course, these names are mentioned *honoris causa* and not in any way to implicate them in any flaws of the final product. Finally, I am grateful for Ellie Haggerty's help in getting the typescript into shape.

1. INTRODUCTION

ORIGINS OF THE U.K. TRIDENT PROGRAM

On December 25, 1991, Mikhail Gorbachev surrendered power in Moscow, and the Union of Soviet Socialist Republics passed into history. Six months later, at their Washington summit, Presidents Bush and Yeltsin agreed on the main features of the subsequent START II Treaty. Plotting the reduction of the superpower strategic arsenals from their then-extant levels of over 10,000 deployable warheads apiece to figures as low as 3,500 to 3,000, this agreement constituted something more than the biggest disarmament deal in history--it also marked the end of nearly fifty years of Cold War. "Today," the U.S. President told his Russian counterpart, "marks the beginning of a new era, a new kind of summit, not a meeting between two powers struggling for global supremacy but between two partners striving to build a democratic peace."

Meanwhile, in March 1992, the first of the United Kingdom's four planned Trident ballistic missile submarines was rolled out of the construction hall at Vickers Shipbuilding and Engineering Limited at Barrow-in-Furness in Cumbria. She was named *Vanguard* by the Princess of Wales at a ceremony the following month. One of Britain's biggest military acquisitions was, it might seem, coming to fruition just at the time when the requirement for it had gone.

Certainly, the U.K. Trident program had been conceived and initiated in a very different world. Planning for the eventual replacement of the U.K. Polaris submarine force had begun in the late 1970s, and U.S. agreement to sell Britain Trident missiles for deployment in a successor force was confirmed in an exchange of letters between President Carter and Prime Minister Thatcher in July 1980. The Carter administration was still feeling the shock of the Soviet invasion of Afghanistan. Earlier deprecation of an "inordinate fear of communism"[1] had given way to acute anxiety about Soviet expansionist intentions, especially in the Southwest Asia "arc of crisis." The

---

[1]See President Carter's commencement address at Notre Dame University, May 22, 1977.

recent Iranian revolution had again demonstrated American and European dependence on Middle East oil in the most vivid fashion, with the return of lines at the gas station. The Russian move into Afghanistan recalled the Great Game of the nineteenth century and the historic Tsarist ambition for direct access to the warm waters of the Indian Ocean. The progressively widening deployments of a growing Soviet blue-water navy were watched with apprehension, while the activity of Soviet "proxy" forces (mainly Cuban and mainly in Africa) was studied for correlation with strategic mineral sources and potential shipping choke points. Communists in Italy and France moved closer to a share in government; and even at the nuclear-strategic level, worries grew about a "window of vulnerability" to Soviet preemptive strike before the new MX and cruise missiles could be brought into service.

Against this background, it was hardly surprising that, having identified Trident as the best replacement for Polaris, the British Government should have determined to proceed with the acquisition; nor, that the U.S. government should have agreed to sell the system to its staunchest European ally (and one which also disposed, in Diego Garcia in the Indian Ocean, of a piece of real estate of inestimable value in underpinning the new Carter doctrine in the Gulf). The sale of the Polaris missile provided the precedent; indeed, the new agreement used the framework of the 1963 Polaris Sales Agreement.

That the Trident decision was made in 1980, only twelve years after the first U.K. Polaris boat had entered service, was a function of the lead time required for so massive an undertaking. Events confirmed the wisdom of this early commitment. The developing program had to accommodate some significant changes in direction: notably, the 1982 decision to purchase the Trident II rather than the Trident I missile system[2] (to ensure continuing commonality with U.S. holdings over the life of the force); and the 1986 decision to conduct all U.K. missile maintenance at the U.S. facility at King's Bay, Georgia (rather than constructing U.K. facilities at the British submarine base at Faslane on

---

[2]The Trident II (D5) missile is newer and bigger than the Trident I (C4), allowing a longer range or a heavier payload--up to 12, as opposed to 8, warheads.

the Clyde, as had been the case for Polaris). The program has proceeded on time and within budget. Nonetheless, *Vanguard* is not due to undertake her first operational deployment until "towards the end of 1994 or early in 1995"[3]--by which time the remainder of the aging Polaris fleet will have been up to 26 years in service. HMS *Revenge*, the first of the four boats to be decommissioned, completed her last patrol in April 1992. In terms of ensuring continuity of the United Kindom strategic deterrent, there was nothing premature about the 1980 commitment to Trident.

These considerations, however, are not enough to dispel a sense, if not of anachronism, at least of infelicity of timing in the arrival of the Trident force--a sense reinforced by the likely near-coincidence of *Vanguard's* first patrol with the watershed 1995 conference to consider the extension of the 1968 Nuclear Non-Proliferation Treaty (NPT). Given that the nuclear issue has been one of the major fault-lines in British politics for at least the last three decades,[4] one might suppose that this combination of circumstances would have returned the question of unilateral nuclear disarmament to the top of the U.K. political agenda. One would, however, suppose wrong. At the very time when the case for U.K. Trident might seem most vulnerable, all three major U.K. political parties are committed to continue the program. The seeming paradox is explained by political--and financial--considerations.

The key political consideration is the widely accepted view that the Labour Party's support for unilateral nuclear disarmament contributed significantly to its defeats in the general elections of 1983 and 1987. Determined not to leave this flank exposed a third time, Neil Kinnock contrived, in the years after 1987, to move his party's official position away from unilateralism to multilateralism. A significant minority then remained (and still remain) committed to the unilateralist cause. However, Labour fought the 1992 general election on the basis of a policy that declared: "We will continue with the

---

[3]*Statement on the Defence Estimates 1994*, Cmnd 2550, London: HMSO, April 1994, p. 35.

[4]For one useful summary of the evolving United Kingdom debate, see Christopher J. Bowie and Alan A. Platt, *British Nuclear Policymaking*, Santa Monica, Calif.: RAND, R-3085-AF, January 1984.

Trident vessels under construction, deploy the boats which are now being
built and continue to operate the existing Polaris fleet. We will
retain nuclear weapons as long as other countries possess them"[5]. With
the Liberal Democrats similarly reaffirming that ". . . the need for a
British minimum deterrent will remain,"[6] there was substantial
congruence[7] between the positions of the three main parties.

This broad consensus was made the easier by the fact that the scope
for saving money by stopping the program was rapidly diminishing. Of
the total program cost of £9,937 million[8] about 84 percent had been
spent or committed by November 1993.[9] The infrastructure element alone,
mainly involving new facilities at the submarine base at Faslane on the
Clyde, and at the neighboring armaments depot at Coulport, is reported
to have constituted the largest construction program in Europe after the
Channel Tunnel. The savings to be had from terminating the project

---

[5]Labour Party policy briefing handbook, February 1992.

[6]*Shared Security*, Liberal Democrat publication, February 1992.

[7]Conservative attempts to "play the defense card"--and in
particular, the card of nuclear defense--in the general election
campaign were largely unsuccessful. Only one such issue achieved any
profile, and that largely on account of its industrial implications:
with three Trident boats already on order, should the contract for the
fourth be confirmed? The government, arguing that a fourth hull would
be essential to ensure that at least one submarine could be maintained
on station at all times (in continuation of the pattern of unbroken
deterrent patrols maintained by the Polaris force since 1969), asserted
its intention to place the order as soon as contract terms could be
finalized. Labour reserved its position, arguing that it would first
need access to all the relevant data. As it turned out, the
Conservatives won the election, though ironically losing Barrow-in-
Furness; and three months later, in July 1992, duly signed the contract
for the fourth Trident boat. At the point of contract signature, about
30 percent of the cost of the boat (some £169 million in funding for
long-lead items) had already been spent.

[8]House of Commons official report, January 20, 1994, Cols. 826-827.
This figure represents the so-called "hybrid estimate," combining
estimates of costs yet to be incurred at 1993-1994 prices with past
payments at historic prices and exchange rates. Updating all elements
to 1993-1994 price levels produces an overall estimate of £11,631
million.

[9]House of Commons Defence Committee, *The Progress of the Trident
Programme, HC 297*, London: HMSO, May 1994, p. vi; hereafter, the "HCDC
1994 Report."

would be insignificant compared with the investment already irretrievably made.

Nor would the system's expected running costs provide decisive incentive for termination. Estimated at an average of some £200 million per annum[10] over the Trident force's expected thirty-year life (including the costs of refits and decommissioning), the sums are only marginally greater than the operating costs of the Polaris force, and represent under 1 percent of the U.K. defense budget.[11] Such sums, though by no means trivial, do not weigh heavily when set against the scale of the sunk costs and the importance long ascribed by successive British governments to the strategic deterrent.

Consensus, of course, is not unanimity. Though the main parties may currently agree on the need for the retention of British nuclear weapons for the foreseeable future, there are significant differences as to the appropriate size of the arsenal required and the extent to which this matter should be negotiable in the interests of disarmament and nonproliferation. Thus Labour, in the run-up to the 1992 general election, complemented their commitment to retain nuclear weapons with the pledge to "use all effective means--through negotiation--to reduce armaments and contribute toward our aim of the elimination of all nuclear weapons in the world"--and to "secure British participation in nuclear disarmament negotiations and place all Britain's nuclear capability into such negotiations."[12] Also, fundamental opposition to continued nuclear possession persists from both the Scottish Nationalist Party (who regard the maintenance of the strategic deterrent on the Clyde as an imposition by London on the people of Scotland) and traditional unilateralist opinion. The easing of East-West tension and the disappearance of the familiar Soviet threat may have taken some psychological wind out of the unilateralists' sails. Yet, these same circumstances have also furnished the unilateralists with a powerful new

---

[10]HCDC 1994 Report, p. vii.

[11]Even allowing for the planned reductions in United Kingdom defense expenditure in coming years, which by IISS (International Institute of Strategic Studies) calculations will reduce the budget to £20.6 billion, at 1993 prices, by 1996.

[12]Labour Party policy briefing handbook, February 1992.

argument. Just who is it, they can fairly ask, that the U.K. deterrent is now supposed to deter--and from what?

With the relationship between Britain and Russia now declared[13] to be one of partnership rather than confrontation, and with this transformation now symbolised by the mutual de-targeting of strategic missiles, these are good questions. Finding good answers to them will be important for Britain's long-term future as a nuclear-weapon state, and may also--as will be argued shortly--have a bearing on wider relations between Britain and the United States. It is therefore with this question, of the rationale for the U.K.'s nuclear deterrent in the post-Cold War world, that this report is primarily concerned. It may help to begin by recalling more precisely the nature of the old rationale, and why it is no longer adequate.

---

[13]See the "Joint Declaration by the President of the Russian Federation and the Prime Minister of the United Kingdom of Great Britain and Northern Ireland," Moscow, February 15, 1994.

2. OLD RATIONALES AND NEW ATTITUDES

The motives that impel any state to acquire nuclear weapons and subsequently to maintain them are likely to be complex and to evolve over time. Britain's own development of the bomb in the years immediately after the Second World War was prompted by an amalgam of fear of Soviet aggression and a sense of entitlement; as a victor in the global conflict, still struggling to preserve the position of a world power, and as a significant contributor to the success of the Manhattan Project, Britain felt it had earned membership in the nuclear "club." The ensuing decades delivered a series of dispiriting lessons about Britain's true weight and position in the world of the latter half of the twentieth century; but nuclear status remained a balm for a bruised national self-esteem, the more effective for its association with the British armed forces, one of a diminishing number of institutions of British life to retain public confidence and respect. Nuclear status could also be argued to provide leverage in international affairs, exemplified by a permanent seat on the U.N. Security Council; and, without bothering with the arcana of deterrence theory, the "man in the street" felt confident that Britain's security was ultimately guaranteed by possession of the bomb. To speak softly and carry a big stick suited British temperament and self-image.

Nonetheless, British governments never felt comfortable in explaining the point and purpose of the U.K. deterrent in solely nationalistic terms. Their French counterparts made no bones about the inextricable connection between France's hard-won nuclear capability and national status and sovereignty. U.K. Ministers, by contrast, showed themselves more comfortable with the concept that the U.K. deterrent was something that the U.K. maintained as much for the benefit of its friends and allies as for itself. All other considerations apart, such a posture had the virtue of representing the U.K.'s nuclear status as something that nonnuclear allies such as the Germans should appreciate, not resent.

In part, this Alliance-oriented concept of the U.K. deterrent has derived from the closeness of U.S.-U.K. nuclear cooperation. Following the passage of the McMahon Act in 1946, Britain had to rely on her own resources in her pursuit of nuclear capability--eventually achieved with the entry into service of the first of the "V-force" strategic bombers, equipped with the Blue Danube free-fall atomic bomb, in 1955. The conclusion in 1958 of the U.S.-U.K. Agreement for Cooperation on the Uses of Atomic Energy for Mutual Defense Purposes (hereafter "the 1958 Agreement") provided the framework for renewed exchanges on nuclear matters of unparalleled intimacy between the United States and the United Kingdom. But, as Article I of the Agreement made plain, the communication and exchange of information between the two governments and the transfer of materials and equipment proceeded on the basis that "the United States and the United Kingdom are participating in an international arrangement for their mutual defense and security and making substantial and material contributions thereto. . . ."

Britain's willingness, and need, to rely on U.S. help was underlined when, in 1960, the Government cancelled the Blue Streak ballistic missile project and announced instead that it would purchase the U.S. Skybolt air-to-surface missile for its V-bombers. The subsequent U.S. decision in late 1962 to cancel Skybolt dismayed London--until Prime Minister Macmillan persuaded President Kennedy, at their meeting at Nassau in December that year, to sell Britain Polaris missiles for a new submarine force instead. The agreement (like the succeeding arrangements to buy Trident) committed Britain to assign its missile submarines to NATO and to target them in accordance with NATO plans--"except where the United Kingdom Government may decide that supreme national interests are at stake, the force will be used for the purposes of international defense of the Western alliance in all circumstances."[1]

But the idea that Britain should maintain its nuclear deterrent primarily as a contribution to collective Western security was not something imposed by the United States as the price of its cooperation.

---

[1] *Joint Communiqué, Bahamas Meetings, December 1962*, Cmnd. 1915, London: HMSO, 1962.

Rather, it was a position that successive British governments willingly adopted--underscoring it, indeed, by emphasizing their commitment to NATO not merely of U.S.-acquired strategic missiles but of the U.K.'s homegrown free-fall bombs as well. Nonetheless, the idea of the U.K. nuclear deterrent as a contribution to collective Alliance security required some explication. With the U.S. nuclear arsenal climbing toward figures in excess of 30,000 warheads,[2] the addition of a few hundred U.K. weapons might seem an insignificant contribution. But numbers, it was argued, were not the point--what gave the U.K. deterrent its particular "value added" was its existence as a second, independent center of nuclear decisionmaking within the Alliance.

Despite the U.S. nuclear guarantee, there was always the risk (or so the argument[3] ran) that the Soviet Union might be tempted into aggression in Europe by the calculation that, in the event, the United States would choose to withold its strategic capability rather than face nuclear retaliation against its homeland. To identify this risk did not involve subscribing to any theory of U.S. unreliability--it was enough to establish that here was a gamble that the Soviets might conceivably be tempted to take. However, in such a scenario the strategists in the Kremlin would also have to take into account how the United Kingdom would react; and they might feel less sanguine about discounting the possibility of nuclear resistance from a European power, arguably more directly threatened by, and certainly geographically much closer to, invasion across Europe's central front. Thus the existence of an independent British (and, indeed, French) nuclear deterrent could be argued to block off one possible chink in the Allied front which an aggressive adversary might otherwise have been tempted to try to exploit.

---

[2]See Thomas B. Cochran, William M. Arkin, and Milton M. Hoenig, *Nuclear Weapons Databook, Volume I*, Cambridge, Mass.: Ballinger Publishing Company, 1984. Table 1.6 estimates that the U.S. nuclear stockpile peaked in 1967 at some 32,000 warheads.

[3]For its best exposition, see Ministry of Defence, *The Future United Kingdom Strategic Deterrent Force*, Defence Open Government Document 80/23, London, 1980.

This rationale was satisfying at various levels. It provided a justification for Britain's position as a nuclear-weapon state in broader and more appealing terms than narrow national self-interest. By tying U.K. nuclear possession specifically to the purposes and missions of the NATO Alliance it guarded the proliferation flank: the justification could be argued to be specific to a particular and limited set of geostrategic circumstances and thus not to "read across" elsewhere. It seized the moral high ground by representing the U.K. deterrent as an integral part of NATO's overall strategy for keeping the peace between East and West; those who urged on moral grounds the abolition of such destructive and indiscriminate weapons could be countered with the argument that what they campaigned against were actually proven instruments of war prevention. And finally, through the second center argument, it identified a specific doctrinal niche for an independent U.K. deterrent--a ready explanation of why friends and allies, especially the United States, should regard the existence of the U.K. deterrent as a net asset to international security.

Clearly, however, the end of the Cold War has undermined this position. The palpable threat to Western Europe has all but evaporated. The demise of the Warsaw Pact, the disintegration of the former Soviet armed forces, and the transformation of the countries of Central and Eastern Europe into a sort of reverse glacis all make the idea of Russian tanks rolling into Germany in the foreseeable future unthinkable. The relaxation of eyeball-to-eyeball confrontation across the Iron Curtain has simply removed the relevance of a rationale based on the premise of a potential credibility gap affecting the U.S. nuclear guarantee to Europe.

Accordingly, in the most recent comprehensive statement of how the British government sees its nuclear policy in the aftermath of the Cold War, some significant repositioning is evident. In a speech on November 16, 1993, at the Centre for Defence Studies at King's College, London, British Defence Secretary Malcolm Rifkind traded heavily on the desirability of preserving a tried-and-trusted framework for peace and security in Europe. There is no talk now of "second centers," or the need to deter Russia (though it is noted that she "will remain the preeminent military power in Europe"). Rather, the suggestion is elliptically made that ". . . decisions about our own future force structures and postures should take into careful account what has proved hitherto to be successful in maintaining stability in the presence of Russia's military strength." The message is essentially conservative: "Having achieved a stable and secure system of war-prevention in the Cold War context, we should be in no hurry to throw away the benefits."

This line of argument is certainly not trivial. "If it ain't bust, don't fix it" is a maxim of enduring value. But it cannot be said to amount to an inspirational rationale--or one which provides compelling reason to ascribe any particular "value-added" to the retention of a specifically British nuclear deterrent. This would perhaps matter less if there were an enduring unanimity of view within the Atlantic Alliance on the continuing value of nuclear deterrence in the post-Cold War world. As it is, a redefinition of the rationale for the British deterrent is made both tougher and more necessary by a fundamental shift in attitudes toward nuclear weapons in the United States.

THE ATLANTIC FAULT LINE

Divergence in European and American attitudes toward nuclear weapons is nothing new.[4] The European view has been framed above all by decades of vulnerability to Soviet conventional power and a profound awareness of the devastation that (even victorious) conventional war in the modern age will wreak. Thus, since 1945, the priority for Europeans has been the deterrence of *all* war on their continent; and if the price for that has had to be a heightened risk of nuclear war, even of

---

[4]European attitudes themselves are, of course, by no means monolithic--any more than they are immune to evolution. There have, for example, always been significant differences of approach and emphasis between, on the one hand, the European nuclear-weapon states (whose independent deterrents have been felt to confer a degree of immunity on their national territories), and on the other, Germany (reliant on others for extended deterrence and the country most likely to suffer nuclear destruction if deterrence had failed). Nonetheless, from that point in the late 1950s when the Soviet attainment of a second-strike capability invalidated the original, straightforward NATO doctrine of massive retaliation for any Soviet aggression in Europe, Europeans and Americans have viewed nuclear weapons and their role in deterrence from rather different perspectives.

apocalyptic strategic nuclear exchange, then the price has been worth
paying. Europeans have, in consequence, tended to favor doctrines and
force postures that have presented the threat of U.S. strategic power to
Soviet leaders in Moscow with the greatest possible "immediacy"--leaving
them no room to discount the ultimate U.S. threat on the ground either
that it was a bluff or that, since it came into play only when
everything else had failed, there would be time enough to deflect it as
war in Western Europe unfolded.

Such attitudes were not, of course, held by Europeans with uniform
consistency over the decades of the Cold War. Periods of concern about
the credibility of the U.S. nuclear guarantee to Europe were intercut
with spasms of anxiety about imagined U.S. trigger-happiness (at least
as far as nuclear use in Europe was concerned). As Wohlstetter observed
in a classic article[5] over thirty years ago, "Europeans do fear that so
drastic a promise might not suffice to deter a carefully prepared
aggression that was clearly at a lower level of violence. They also
fear that if the aggression occurred we might keep our promise." To
Kissinger, European attitudes reflected a preference for having a
nuclear war, if one occurred, fought between the United States and the
Soviet Union over their heads.[6] Certainly, the European interest was
always in a short, conspicuous powder trail from initial aggression to
the U.S. strategic arsenal.

Unsurprisingly, a different history and different geostrategic
situation produced different U.S. attitudes. Since the Civil War, the
United States has had no experience of sustained warfare on its
territory. For well over a century, geographic position and economic
and military power rendered the U.S. homeland effectively immune from
external threat--from the Republic's earliest days to the advent of the
atomic era. (Pearl Harbor aside, the last major violation of U.S.
territory occurred in 1812 when the British burned Washington--at much
the same moment that the French were burning Moscow.) Soviet nuclear

---

[5]Albert Wohlstetter, "Nuclear Sharing: NATO and the N + 1
Country," *Foreign Affairs*, April 1961.
[6]Henry A. Kissinger, *White House Years*, Boston: Little, Brown and
Company, 1979, p. 219.

capability forced an initial acceptance of the doctrine of Mutual Assured Destruction, but there could be no question of the United States reconciling itself to this new and total vulnerability.

This urge to be rid of this single, deadly vulnerability found eloquent expression when Ronald Reagan launched[7] his *Strategic Defense Initiative* in 1983--and took him to the verge of agreeing with Gorbachev at the 1986 Reykjavik Summit on the complete elimination of nuclear weapons. Other Americans have taken a less ambitious approach, accepting that continuing nuclear commitment to the defense of Europe provided a better chance of managing the threat than would isolationism, but seeking to structure deterrent arrangements in such a way as to minimize the likelihood of the United States becoming involved in intercontinental nuclear exchanges. The recurring U.S. themes have been the need to bolster conventional defense in Europe so as to "raise the nuclear threshold" (as, for example, with the Carter 1977 Long Term Defense Plan) and to develop concepts for limited nuclear use in Europe that, by engaging U.S. strategic power, might obviate the need to risk the U.S. homeland.

The history of the development of NATO strategy has in large measure been the history of the management of this transatlantic tension. Michael Legge has described how "Flexible Response," adopted by the Alliance in 1967, derived from the need to reconcile divergent U.S. and European attitudes. The strategy left ambiguous how NATO might choose to react to any particular attack; "a degree of ambiguity was also necessary in order to allow the American and European Allies sufficient scope to interpret the strategy in accordance with their own preoccupations and perspectives." The Alliance's reservation of the right to initiate nuclear use with theater nuclear weapons (TNW) in response to Soviet aggression was acceptable to both parties "for essentially contradictory reasons: the Europeans, because the threat to use TNW represented the best way of "coupling" the U.S. strategic

---

[7]In a nationally televised address on peace and national security on March 23, 1983, Reagan called upon "the scientific community who gave us nuclear weapons to turn their great talents to the cause of mankind and world peace: to give us the means of rendering these weapons impotent and obsolete."

deterrent to the defense of Europe; and the Americans, because it offered the best hope of preventing a major land battle in Europe from escalating to an all-out strategic exchange."[8]

Flexible Response was a sophisticated compromise, providing a framework within which conflicting Alliance views[9] were satisfactorily reconciled for almost a quarter of a century. But a strategy for keeping the peace in a divided Europe could have little hope of surviving unscathed the dissolution of communist regimes in Eastern Europe and the prospect of a unified Germany--as NATO's London Summit in July 1990 recognized. The London Declaration on a Transformed Atlantic Alliance offered the members of the still-just-extant Warsaw Treaty Organization the formal end of an adversarial relationship; presaged the end of "substrategic nuclear systems of the shortest range" (i.e., nuclear artillery and Lance missiles); and announced the preparation of a new strategy "modifying flexible response to reflect a reduced reliance on nuclear weapons."

The elaboration that this new strategy would make nuclear weapons "truly weapons of last resort"[10] was promptly seized on by more Gaullist

---

[8]J. Michael Legge, *Theater Nuclear Weapons and the NATO Strategy of Flexible Response*, Santa Monica, Calif.: RAND, R-2964-FF, April 1983.

[9]Excepting, of course, the French, who found it convenient to parody the strategy as a process of slow escalation entailing the devastation of Europe while U.S. strategic power was withheld--in contrast, of course, with their own doctrine of "last warning" ("ultime avertissement") which was claimed to underline the immediacy of the connection between first nuclear use and holocaust.

[10]The full text of paragraph 18 of the declaration, which elaborates the "New Concept," is of interest:

"Finally with the total withdrawal of Soviet stationed forces and the implementation of a CFE (Conventional Forces in Europe) agreement, the Allies concerned can reduce their reliance on nuclear weapons. These will continue to fulfill an essential role in the overall strategy of the Alliance to prevent war by ensuring that there are no circumstances in which nuclear retaliation in response to military action might be discounted. However, in the transformed Europe, they will be able to adopt a new NATO strategy making nuclear weapons truly weapons of last resort."

Perhaps the most striking feature of this language (apart from the curious use of the intensive "truly" before "last resort") is the elements in France as new evidence of the United States' inner bias toward standing aside from European conflict--which explains why, when the new strategy[11] itself emerged, the offending phrase had disappeared. The New Concept manages to associate "reduced reliance" with the uncontroversial observation that an improving security environment means that "the circumstances in which any use of nuclear weapons might have to be contemplated . . . are even more remote"--and with the judgment that deterrence could be preserved with a smaller number of nuclear weapons in Europe.

Formal Alliance harmony[12] was restored. But the reality remained that many in the United States had perceived in the end of the Cold War an historic opportunity to get the monkey of nuclear vulnerability off its back. The incentive to do so was greatly reinforced by the success of U.S. arms in the Gulf War against Saddam Hussein.

NEW U.S. ATTITUDES

The dramatic success of the campaign conducted between January 17, and February 28, 1991, to liberate Kuwait from Iraqi occupation had a

---

disjunction between the second and third sentences. If there are "no circumstances in which nuclear retaliation . . . might be discounted" (itself a rather implausible thought, even in earlier times when massive in-place forces confronted each other across the inner-German border), then how can nuclear weapons be described as weapons of last resort? The linking adverb "however" is required to bear an unsupportable load.

This paragraph thus provides an intriguing glimpse of the reopening of old divides within the Alliance, as between the U.S. and Europe (or, to be more precise in relation to these specific sentences, as between the U.S. president and the British prime minister) over fundamental attitudes to nuclear weapons. As noted above, "last resort" was omitted from the finished strategy in deference to the political stir the phrase had created. Omitted, too, was "no circumstances," perhaps in deference to common sense.

[11]*The Alliance's Strategic Concept*, published at the Rome meeting of the North Atlantic Council on November 7, 1991.

[12]Even the French found themselves able to subscribe to most of this new document (their abstentions on certain nuclear elements, signified by the formula "the Allies concerned," having less to do with nuclear theology than with their unwillingness to endorse language about the obsolescence of short-range systems that would have condemned their new Hades missile along with the Lance).

profound effect upon U.S. military and strategic thinking. It gave conclusive confirmation, in a way for which the operations of the previous decade in Grenada and Panama had not sufficed, that after Vietnam, U.S. military power was back. Moreover, the extraordinarily one-sided nature of the campaign, after all the initial apprehensions, seemed to demonstrate a degree of preeminence that no other power on earth could match.

The realization that the United States was now, for the first time in history, the undisputed military champion of the world, cast a new light on the role and utility of nuclear weapons. The change was lucidly expressed by the then Congressman Aspin, Chairman of the House Armed Services Committee, in a paper he produced early in 1992.[13] Aspin affirmed:

> During the Cold War, the United States and its NATO allies relied on nuclear weapons to offset the conventional superiority of the Warsaw Pact in Europe. Even a few years ago, if someone had offered the United States a magic wand that could have instantly wiped out all nuclear weapons and the knowledge to make more of them, the reality is we would have declined the offer. Nuclear weapons were the great equalizer that enabled Western capitals to deal with numerically larger Eastern Bloc forces. . . . Today, however, circumstances are dramatically different. With the disappearance of the Warsaw Pact and the fading of the threat posed by former Soviet forces, the United States is the biggest conventional force on the block. Nuclear weapons still serve the same purpose--as a great equalizer. But it is the United States that is now the potential equalizee. . . . Today, if offered that magic wand to eradicate the existence and knowledge of nuclear weapons, we would very likely accept it.

Another lesson was to be drawn from the Gulf campaign--the dangers posed by nuclear proliferation. As the international community pursued the selective disarmament of Iraq, it became clear that Western intelligence agencies had seriously underestimated the scale of Saddam Hussein's programs to produce a nuclear weapon, and the progress he had

---

[13]Representative Les Aspin, Chairman, House Armed Services Committee, *From Deterrence to Denuking: Dealing with Proliferation in the 1990s*, February 18, 1992.

made. The thought of how an Iraqi nuclear weapon might have affected the operational conduct of the Desert Storm campaign and the coherence of the coalition against Iraq was worrisome. At the very moment when the historic Soviet menace was receding, a new threat, of unconstrained nuclear proliferation, seemed to have emerged to take its place. It might not hold out the same, immediate risk to the U.S. homeland as its predecessor; but it was Hydra-headed, could only grow with time, and even in the short term threatened to trump America's just-won conventional supremacy. Moreover, the collapse of the Soviet Union itself heightened the proliferation risk. Nuclear weapons in Ukraine, Belarus, and Kazakhstan might be appropriated by the new national authorities, while the loss of central control over the former Soviet Union's nuclear infrastructure might result in expertise, materials, or, conceivably, even whole weapons migrating into the hands of would-be proliferators with the money to pay for them.[14]

The start of the last decade of the twentieth century thus seemed pregnant with opportunity and risk. The dilemma was how to achieve Aspin's "magic wand" effect in a world without magic--and a substantial literature has developed in the United States over the past two or three years on how the role of nuclear weapons in international security affairs could, and/or should, be attenuated.

Arguably, indeed, the intellectual germ of the theme can be found in the previous decade. Patrick Garrity, in his own contribution on "The Depreciation of Nuclear Weapons in International Politics,"[15] credits Edward Luttwak with the proclamation of the end of the nuclear era in 1988. By the Fall 1991 edition of *Foreign Affairs*, Carl Kaysen, Robert McNamara, and George Rathjens were asking why the United States should not "lead or at least join others in a move for the abolition of all nuclear weapons."

---

[14]For a good analysis of the risks, see Kurt M. Campbell et al., *Soviet Nuclear Fission: Control of the Nuclear Arsenal in a Disintegrating Soviet Union*, Cambridge, Mass.: Center for Science and International Affairs, John F. Kennedy School of Government, Harvard University, 1991.

[15]Patrick J. Garrity, "The Depreciation of Nuclear Weapons in International Affairs: Possibilities, Limits, Uncertainties," *The Journal of Strategic Studies*, December 1991.

An even more explicitly millenarian note was struck by the *Bulletin of the Atomic Scientists*, in devoting its May 1992 edition to a range of contributions on the role of nuclear weapons in the year 2001 and beyond. Rejecting the conventional punctuation of the history of the twentieth century, which places a colon in late 1945 and regards the ensuing 45 or so years as constituting a discrete atomic-age clause, the editor boldly announced that "The Great Ninety Years War--which began with the posturing of imperial powers in Europe at the turn of the century, and which produced two world wars, the East-West nuclear arms race, the worldwide political and economic distortions of the Cold War, and a host of brutal regional conflicts--is over." Paul Warnke's contribution to this *Bulletin*, "Missionless Missiles," was a powerful statement of the abolitionist's credo: "Looking forward to the world we want for 2001, the United States should underscore--not repudiate--the policy that U.S. nuclear weapons are designed exclusively to prevent nuclear attack . . . the kinds of conflicts we can anticipate are not ones in which nuclear weapons can play a constructive role. Only by devaluing them--stripping them of their special-status symbolism--can we avoid the risk that regional conflicts and civil wars will be rendered exponentially more dreadful by the spread of nuclear weapons . . . the United States should be trumpeting the military uselessness of such weapons and declaring a firm no-first-use policy."

Comparable statements could be cited at some length.[16] Of course, similar arguments are not unheard in the United Kingdom.[17] What,

---

[16]See, for example, the sizeable literature on "conventional deterrence" briefly reviewed in Section 5. Other notable recent contributions to the debate have come from McGeorge Bundy, William Crowe, and Sidney Drell, writing in the Spring 1993 issue of *Foreign Affairs* on "Reducing Nuclear Danger" (for a fuller version of the same authors' views, see *Reducing Nuclear Danger: The Road Away from the Brink*, New York: Council on Foreign Relations, 1993); and from Robert A. Levine in *Uniform Deterrence of Nuclear First Use*, Santa Monica, Calif.: RAND, MR-231-CC, 1993. Levine explores the idea that the United States, acting less as global policeman than as global sheriff organizing a posse of likeminded powers, might aim to deter any further nuclear use by the pledge of "punishment by appropriate military action" of any future perpetrator. He makes no bones that this approach is incompatible with the reservation of the right of first use, as in current NATO strategy, and "is based on the axiom that protecting the

however, strikes the European observer is the extent to which this
tendency to reject the legitimacy and utility of nuclear weapons now
seems to dominate the mainstream of U.S. thinking on strategic issues.
It has become, in both senses, the new conventional wisdom. Nor is the
prevalence of the approach something confined to academic circles. Even
more striking is to see public figures of the distinction and experience
of Paul Nitze[18] and Colin Powell[19] lending their authority to the theme.

    The lesson, it seems, has been widely learned. In a recent study
of options for containing proliferation, Roger Molander and Peter

---

firebreak--avoiding any use of any nuclear weapons by anyone--should be
at the top of the list of U.S. and world priorities."

    [17]See, for example, Michael MccGwire, "Is There a Future for
Nuclear Weapons?" *International Affairs*, Vol. 70, No. 2, 1994.
Similarly, Michael Clarke, "British and French Nuclear Forces After the
Cold War", *Arms Control*, April 1993, writes that "the 1990s may
represent the last good opportunity to denuclearize the world" and
argues that British and French disarmament could "promote optimistic
nonproliferation." Also, Ken Booth and Nicholas Wheeler, "Beyond
Nuclearism," in Regina Cowen Karp, ed., *Security Without Nuclear
Weapons?* Oxford: Oxford University Press, 1992, discern a new "scope to
change the strategic culture of world politics," and urge that "the goal
of global nuclear elimination is therefore crucial." But the other side
of the argument is equally well represented in the recent literature--
as, for example, with Michael Quinlan's "The Future of Nuclear Weapons:
Policy for the Western Possessors," *International Affairs*, Vol. 69, No.
3, 1993, or Colin Gray's "Through a Missile Tube Darkly: 'New Thinking'
About Nuclear Strategy," *Political Studies*, December 1993, in which,
having cast a sceptical eye over the "new thinking," he cautions "that a
prudent realism and 'old thinking' won the Cold War, but that nothing
can fail like success," since "no sooner does realism succeed, than its
post-war legitimacy is undermined." And Lawrence Freedman, "Britain and
Nuclear Weapons," in Michael Clarke and Philip Sabin, eds., *British
Defence Choices for the Twenty-First Century*, London and New York:
Brassey's, 1993, concludes that "The residual threat may be remote and
defy precise identification, but nuclear strategy has always been geared
to remote scenarios," and that "Nuclear weapons can play the role that
they have always played--of reminding of the folly of total war--but in
circumstances less demanding than before."

    [18]"Is it Time to Junk Our Nukes? The New World Disorder Makes Them
Obsolete," *The Washington Post*, January 16, 1994, p. C1.

    [19]"I also think nuclear weapons have much less political utility
than anyone thinks they do. . . ." One of two similar remarks by Powell
quoted by Marc Dean Millot in "Facing New Nuclear Adversaries," *The
Washington Quarterly*, Summer 1994, p. 53.

Wilson[20] record the results of a series of games they have conducted, with the participation of U.S. administration officials and serving officers as well as defense analysts and observers, designed to illuminate the part that nuclear weapons could play (on either side) in a range of future crises or conflicts, and then to relate the insights thus derived to the current development of nuclear policy in the "real world." The results of the initial round of these games point up not only the military intractability[21] of dealing with a successful proliferator, but also the reluctance of U.S. players to contemplate use of their own nuclear weapons, even in retaliation, on the grounds that any such resort would "send the wrong message" about the utility and legitimacy of nuclear weapons in the post-Cold War environment.

That the prevailing intellectual climate should be reflected in official attitudes is not surprising--especially when several of the Clinton administration's key members have been influential in forming it. Les Aspin's views have already been noted; his successor as Defense Secretary has also written about "a radical deemphasis of nuclear weapons in the security conceptions of the major powers," whereby "doctrines covering the residual nuclear forces . . . would foresee retaliation only, and that only in response to first nuclear use."[22]

---

[20]*The Nuclear Asymptote: On Containing Nuclear Proliferation*, Santa Monica, Calif.: RAND, MR-214-CC, 1993. For a summary version, see, by the same authors, "On Dealing with the Prospect of Nuclear Chaos," *The Washington Quarterly*, Summer 1994. One option considered is "Virtual Abolition," whereby the arsenals of the five officially recognized nuclear-weapon states would be cut back to only a few hundreds, or even tens, of warheads. The authors remark that "The Virtual Abolition option reflects a view that in the post-Cold War world, the United States and other nuclear-armed nations could--and maybe in their own long-term interests should--abandon their current degree of dependence on nuclear weapons."

[21]The authors note among the U.S. military "a rapidly growing appreciation that a small nuclear arsenal in the hands of a regional predator (such as Iraq in 1991) would present any U.S. or U.S.-led military force with a daunting and possibly technically insoluble set of basic military problems."

[22]Ashton B. Carter, William J. Perry, and John D. Steinbruner, *A New Concept of Cooperative Security*, Washington, D.C.: The Brookings Institution, 1992.

This piece was coauthored with Ashton Carter who elsewhere[23] (writing with Harvard colleagues) well expressed the theme of historic opportunity. "The end of the Cold War and disappearance of the Soviet Union have brought the international community to a fateful fork in the road. Down one path lies the elimination of nuclear weapons from the central role they have played in international life for 50 years. At this crossroad, however, a second path leads to a quite different twenty-first century. . . . Down this second path, a dramatic spread of nuclear weapons, in new and dangerous forms, could dominate the early decades of a new century." If the opportunity is seized, the authors argue, "the reduction and strengthened control of nuclear arsenals would be accompanied by a reduction in the political salience of nuclear weapons. As the great powers turned away from reliance on nuclear weapons, they would set a better example for other nations that might be tempted to turn to nuclear weapons in the belief that they provide military security."

The same sense of a fateful crossroad in world affairs informed President Clinton's first major statement of his foreign policy, in an address to the United Nations General Assembly on September 27, 1993. Referring to "a new era of peril and opportunity," he recalled the occasion 32 years earlier when President Kennedy had warned the same audience that "humanity lived under a nuclear sword of Damocles that hung by the slenderest of threads." He noted the efforts the United States was making, in conjunction with the states of the former Soviet Union, "to take that sword down, to lock it away in a secure vault where we hope and pray that it will remain forever." But success could not be taken for granted; "we must confront the storm clouds that may overwhelm our work and darken the march toward freedom. If we do not stem the proliferation of the world's deadliest weapons, no democracy can feel secure." Accordingly, the president declared, "I have made nonproliferation one of our nation's highest priorities."

---

[23]Graham Allison, Ashton B. Carter, Steven E. Miller, and Philip Zelikow, eds., *Cooperative Denuclearization--from Pledges to Deeds*, Cambridge, Mass.: Center for Science and International Affairs, John F. Kennedy School of Government, Harvard University, 1993.

3. THE POTENTIAL FOR FRICTION

DENUCLEARIZATION AND NONPROLIFERATION

Neither of the two main policy thrusts deriving from this revivified U.S. determination to reduce nuclear danger has presented the United Kingdom with any particular difficulty. "Taking down the sword of Damocles" has in practice meant a new concentration on efforts to help the states of the former Soviet Union, principally Russia, with the vast task of nuclear dismantlement they face. The two START (Strategic Arms Reduction Talks) agreements, along with the various unilateral undertakings of 1991 and 1992 on reduction of tactical nuclear weapons, have left a surplus of warheads in the former Soviet Union that even the most conservative estimates put at upwards of 20,000. The true figure could be very much higher;[1] and earlier assessments that Russian facilities should be adequate to complete the dismantlement task in perhaps ten or a dozen years may have similarly been significantly over-optimistic.

There is therefore a very obvious Western interest in doing whatever is possible to accelerate the process, and to minimize the chances of weapons or their constituents ending up in the wrong hands. Though the United States has taken the main lead the United Kingdom has contributed usefully, agreeing with the Russian authorities on a $50 million program for the supply of special safe-and -secure trucks and containers for the transport of nuclear warheads to their place of disassembly. In dealings with Ukraine, London lent diplomatic support by associating the United Kingdom with the contingent security assurances that helped President Kravchuk reach agreement with Presidents Clinton and Yeltsin in January 1994 over the transfer of strategic weapons to Russia.

---

[1]References by the Russian minister of atomic energy to an overall arsenal size of some 45,000 warheads in the late 1980s imply that the best Western estimates may have been as much as 18,000 too low; see "Russian Says Soviet Atom Arsenal Was Larger than West Estimated," *New York Times*, September 26, 1993, p. A1.

Transatlantic harmony has also prevailed on the importance of inhibiting nuclear proliferation in the wider world. In his landmark paper, "The Spread of Nuclear Weapons: More May Be Better," Kenneth Waltz argued that the deterrent, war-preventing properties of nuclear arsenals as identified in the context of East-West Cold War confrontation should equally well apply in other regions and circumstances; "the measured spread of nuclear weapons is more to be welcomed than feared."[2] The argument has since been repeatedly rerun in academic circles, for recent example by John Mearsheimer in relation to Ukraine.[3]

There has, however, been no disposition in Western government circles to encourage, or even to acquiesce in, the testing of this theory in practice. Not only has the proferred end-state seemed highly undesirable (even limited further proliferation could well put nuclear weapons into the hands of Iraq and Iran, either or both of whom would then be predictably emboldened to act in ways contrary to Western interests), but the process too has seemed fraught with risk. Further war between a nuclear-armed Iraq and a similarly equipped Iran might indeed be less likely than if neither is able to obtain such weapons; but, since simultaneous acquisition is improbable, the chances must be considered fairly high that whichever of those two rival states got there first would attempt to exploit the fact for decisive advantage over the other. Nor could a situation of mutual deterrence between those two countries, even supposing it to be achieved, be regarded as a net factor for stability, given the enormous pressures that would then be engendered in Damascus, in Riyadh, and even in Cairo to follow suit-- and given the consequent pressures that would be engendered elsewhere in the region to anticipate or to prevent such significant further shifts in the regional balance of power.

Other considerations, too, make nuclear proliferation a deeply unattractive prospect viewed from Western capitals. One is the huge

---

[2]Kenneth N. Waltz, *The Spread of Nuclear Weapons: More May Be Better*, Adelphi Paper No. 171, London: International Institute of Strategic Studies, 1981.
   [3]John J. Mearsheimer, "The Case for a Ukrainian Nuclear Deterrent," *Foreign Affairs*, Summer 1993.

asymmetry between the potentially catastrophic consequences if the Waltz theory proved wrong, and the relatively modest benefits (from the Western perspective) if it proved correct. Another is the heightened risk as nuclear weapons spread if not of accidental use, then of seepage of the capability, into the hands of terrorists or other subnational groups who could not be expected to behave with that circumspection upon which the Waltz thesis depends. In fact, the undesirability of further proliferation of nuclear weapons is an issue upon which there is an almost unparalleled degree of international consensus.[4]

Thus, London has been as willing to follow a renewed U.S. lead against proliferation as it has been to back denuclearization efforts in the former Soviet Union. It is in the *reflexive* elements of the new U.S. approach to nuclear weapons--those parts of policy that deal with what *we,* not with what someone else, should do--that the potential for friction lies. Again, the Aspin paper of February 1992 posed the issues with great clarity: "There has been a fundamental shift in our security interests regarding nuclear weapons. In the deterrence era, we needed nuclear weapons to deter strategic attack on the United States and to deter an overwhelming conventional attack in Europe. In the postdeterrence era, the incentives are reversed. It would be in our interest to get rid of nuclear weapons. In the deterrence era, the burden of proof was on anyone who wanted to shift away from policies supporting U.S. nuclear weapons. Today, the burden of proof is shifting toward those who want to maintain those policies in light of the changed world. Therefore, opposition to the Comprehensive Test Ban Treaty (CTBT), to the further production of fissile materials for new weapons, to the forward deployment of tactical nuclear weapons in Europe, and, above all, to the threat of nuclear-first use are up for reconsideration."

This was a radical agenda, unwelcome to the British government not only in its particulars but in two more fundamental ways. First, it

---

[4]Compare the unanimous declaration by the U.N. Security Council on January 31, 1992, at heads of government level, that proliferation constituted a threat to international peace and security; and compare the 164 (as of April 1994) signatories of the NPT.

represented a concept of the role of nuclear weapons in international affairs wholly different from that to which the British government remained committed. The task of finding a satisfying new account of the purpose of the U.K. deterrent in the post-Cold War world would be made no easier if basic axioms about the value of nuclear weapons came in for challenge. Second, it implied the risk that nuclear issues, long one of the strongest bonds in the wider Anglo-American relationship, might in time become a source as much of discord as of cohesion. Both points deserve explication.

THE ROLE OF NUCLEAR WEAPONS: "BLESSING IN DISGUISE" OR "ULTIMATE EVIL"?

As we have seen, though the "second center of decisionmaking" rationale may have faded, the present British government seems, determined to continue to account for the British deterrent within a conceptual framework that ascribes to nuclear weapons a positive role in underpinning security and stability between nations. In the words of the new NATO Strategic Concept, "Nuclear weapons make a unique contribution in rendering the risks of any aggression incalculable and unacceptable. Thus they remain essential to preserve peace." The argument, in essence, is that nuclear weapons (in the right hands, under the right circumstances, and with the right doctrine--all vital caveats) may be uniquely effective instruments not of warfighting but of war prevention. Their awesome power has brought it home to military establishments that there could be no winners in a nuclear war--in Sir Michael Quinlan's words, they render war between developed nuclear powers "a logical absurdity."[5] Thus they can deter not only nuclear aggression, but *any* kind of aggression that could foreseeably escalate to nuclear levels. Europe's long peace since the Second World War is adduced as evidence of this thesis.

This view is not incompatible with an acute awareness of--indeed, it may be said to depend on it--the dangers of nuclear war. Its adherents may well support the elimination of nuclear overarmament, the relaxation of hair-trigger force postures, and the introduction of all

---

[5]Michael Quinlan, "Nuclear Weapons and the Abolition of War," *International Affairs*, Vol. 67, No. 2, 1991.

manner of fail-safe control mechanisms. They may well oppose the further spread of nuclear weaponry (into the wrong hands, and/or circumstances). But, in circumstances where they judge that existing nuclear capabilities contribute to deterrence and war prevention, they will argue that those capabilities should properly be regarded as net assets to international security. Indeed, we may for convenience label this the Blessing in Disguise view.

It follows that the abolition of nuclear weapons--even discounting all the practical difficulties--is not a goal to which adherents of this view would wish to subscribe. Or, perhaps more accurately, if they did subscribe to it they would do so only in the Utopian context of the elimination of all other instruments of warfare (that is, "pursuant to a treaty on general and complete disarmament under strict and effective international control," as the preamble to the NPT has it). Short of this ideal state, adherents of the Blessing in Disguise school will tend to oppose any constraint on the scope for nuclear weapons (in the right hands and circumstances) to exercise their caution-inducing influence and deter aggression at all levels, nonnuclear as well as nuclear. They will therefore reject the idea of "no first use" declarations (the whole purpose of which, in a sense, would be to establish that nonnuclear aggression would not meet with nuclear sanction), or any other attempts to circumscribe the field of application of nuclear deterrence. They will see no particular virtue (indeed quite possibly the opposite) in measures such as test bans or fissile material cutoffs--compare the Aspin agenda above--that would tend to hamper the capabilities of existing nuclear possessors, unless they can be convinced that they will also hamper proliferators.

This traditional view--still widely found in Europe--contrasts fundamentally with the newly received wisdom in the United States, as so clearly laid out in the Aspin paper. For convenience, we may label this contrasting attitude the Ultimate Evil view, since its central tenet is that nuclear weapons are uniquely dangerous and repugnant. They alone of all instruments of war have the capacity to destroy humankind. There is therefore no more important objective of policy than to try to ensure that they are never used again. Everything should be done to try to reinforce the taboo against their use, to marginalize their relevance to international affairs, and to pursue their elimination as far as it can practically be taken. All possible restraints should be applied to their development, testing, production and deployment, as well as their use. Their only proper role is in the deterrence of nuclear use by others--a tenet that nuclear possessors could greatly reinforce with their declaration of "no first use." The abolition of nuclear weapons may, in practice, not be possible, but if it could somehow be engineered, this would constitute a net benefit to humankind, even if the loss of the potential deterrent to some future Stalin or practitioner of biological warfare is acknowledged. If the "magic wand" could be waved, adherents of this view would not hesitate to do so.

As discussed above, conventional U.S. opinion has now moved much closer to the Ultimate Evil than to the Blessing in Disguise view of nuclear weapons. In doing so, it has diverged from the received wisdom in Europe (at least in governmental circles in Britain and France) and from the axioms that continue to underlie NATO strategy. It is creating an intellectual climate in which the value to international security of Britain's retention of nuclear weapons in the post-Cold War world is less likely to be taken as read--and in which the political charge of the U.S.-U.K. interaction on nuclear issues risks changing from positive to neutral, or even to negative.

THE NUCLEAR DIMENSION OF ANGLO-AMERICAN RELATIONS

As noted above, nuclear cooperation between the United States and the United Kingdom is grounded in the 1958 Agreement--which bases the relationship on participation by both parties in "an international arrangement for their mutual defense and security" and on the continued production by both of "substantial and material contributions thereto." The basic agreement is of indefinite duration; but, as amended in 1959,[6] certain key provisions relating to the transfer of materials, equipment,

---

[6]*Amendment to the Agreement Between the Government of the United Kingdom of Great Britain and Northern Ireland and the Government of the United States of America for Co-operation on the Use of Atomic Energy for Mutual Defence Purposes of July 3, 1958--Washington, May 7, 1959,* London: Her Majesty's Stationery Office, Cmnd 733, May 1959.

and technology are subject to periodic renewal--and thus call for a conscious stocktaking by both parties as to whether the operation of the Agreement is continuing to serve its own national interests. A ten-year extension was agreed in 1984. As the Clinton administration settled into office, London was aware that the renewal process would have to be undertaken again in 1994.

For the United Kingdom, the issue was of great importance. Like the Lord, the U.S. helps those who help themselves, and a fundamental principle of U.S. technical assistance to the United Kingdom over the years has been to provide help only in those areas in which the United Kingdom has demonstrated that it has the means to acquire the competence for itself. Indeed, it was the successful British test of their first, independently developed hydrogen bomb in 1957 that paved the way for the 1958 Agreement. But this is not to disparage the value of the cooperation from the U.K. perspective. On the contrary, the leverage obtained for the comparatively slender U.K. resources devoted to nuclear research and development has been enormous.[7] As only one example, U.K. use of the Nevada Test Site for all its nuclear testing from 1963 onward saved the United Kingdom huge costs that would otherwise have had to be

---

[7]The full extent of the benefit to the United Kingdom is hard to quantify, not least because the published U.K. defense budget has always been reticent about expenditure on the nuclear program. Nonetheless, some interesting comparisons can be drawn with the French experience. The evidence, reviewed Appendix A, suggests that the resource burden on Britain of maintaining its nuclear capability, in cooperation with the United States, has been strikingly modest compared with that incurred by France's autarkic approach. Given defense budgets of similar size--NATO figures indicate that on average over the four years between 1990 to 1993, France's defense expenditure was a little less than 10 percent higher than the U.K.'s--the true costs of France's nuclear burdens may be viewed as an opportunity lost in terms of less capable conventional forces. The difference in British and French conventional capabilities was clearly pointed up in the two nations' respective contributions to the 1991 Gulf War against Saddam Hussein. See, for example, David S. Yost, "France and the Gulf War of 1990-1991: Political-Military Lessons Learned," *The Journal of Strategic Studies*, September 1993. General H. Norman Schwarzkopf also recounts in his autobiography, *It Doesn't Take a Hero*, New York: Bantam Books, 1992, how the positioning of French ground forces on the coalition's extreme left flank in Desert Storm stemmed from French concern that their units were inadequately armoured to oppose the Iraqis' heavy Soviet tanks.

expended on a U.K. national test site--savings only partially offset by the payment of fees to the United States for access to Nevada.

The United Kingdom, then, is heavily dependent for its continuing role as a nuclear-weapon state on the United States--not in the sense that it cannot use its nuclear weapons without U.S. assistance, nor yet in the sense that it would be technically incapable of managing without U.S. help, but in the sense that were U.S. cooperation to be withdrawn, the cost implications for the United Kingdom of staying in the nuclear business would be very severe. Thus, looking ahead to 1994 and contemplating what was potentially at stake in the 1958 Agreement extension, London could have been forgiven a little nervousness. No new U.S. president should be taken for granted; and the necessary presidential determination that "In light of our previous close cooperation and the fact that the United Kingdom has committed its nuclear forces to NATO, I have concluded that it is in our interest to continue to assist them in maintaining a credible nuclear force"[8] might seem less obvious to the head of an administration keen to see nuclear weapons marginalized than it had to his predecessor in the depths of the Cold War.

Any apprehensions on this score, however, will have been allayed by the reflection that, even in the transformed post-Cold War environment, the new administration would recognize that hardheaded U.S. national interest continued to be well-served by the cooperative arrangements. At the technical level, the scope thus provided for "peer review"--for U.S. nuclear specialists to test their judgments and ideas against a knowledgeable sounding-board--would become all the more important with the end of nuclear testing. There were also powerful economic incentives. U.S. assistance to the United Kingdom, whether in the form of services provided by the U.S. nuclear weapons laboratories, of provision of materials, or of access to testing facilities, is all paid for. At the U.K.'s request, these costs remain classified--but not

---

[8]The key sentence in President Reagan's Message to the U.S. Congress of June 6, 1984, transmitting the amendment to extend the provisions of the 1958 Agreement until the end of 1994--and reproduced verbatim in President Clinton's similar Message of May 23, 1994, notifying his approval of a further ten-year extension.

those of the United Kingdom's expenditure in the United States for the
U.K. Trident program. Some 30 percent[9] of the overall program cost,
i.e., well over $5 billion at 1993-1994 prices, is expected to be spent
in the United States--mainly on the strategic missiles themselves and
their associated equipment. The program is thus of considerable
economic significance, in particular to the aerospace-dependent and
recession-hit economy of California.

More broadly, nuclear cooperation, along with the similarly close
relationship in intelligence matters, has long lain at the heart of the
U.S.-U.K. "special relationship." Neither party may now attach to this
phenomenon the importance it once did, but that should not obscure the
enduring value to the United States of a continuing British
predisposition to be helpful--a predisposition evinced both through
habitual sympathy with U.S. aims and understanding of U.S. needs, and
through more concrete forms of strategic support, such as the provision
of bases and staging facilities. Any U.S. refusal to continue nuclear
cooperation could have thrown all this away, in the biggest rupture
between London and Washington since the 1956 Suez crisis.[10] Against
this background London will have been gratified, but not surprised, when
President Clinton approved the extension of the 1958 Agreement.

THE POTENTIAL FOR ANGLO-AMERICAN DISCORD

Nonetheless, the perception by both parties of strong national
advantage in continuing technical cooperation does nothing to guarantee
that the special intimacy of past relations in the field of broader
nuclear policy will endure. On the contrary, the de-emphasizing of
nuclear weapons in the NATO Alliance and, more generally, in the
security policy of the West, must inevitably make this particular form
of U.S.-U.K. interaction count for less. In addition, the divergence
noted above of underlying attitudes toward nuclear weapons suggests that
nuclear issues may for the future have the potential to inject as much

---

[9]HCDC 1994 Report, p. 23.

[10]Anyone needing evidence of the British sensitivity to being left
in the nuclear lurch by the United States will only have had to recall
London's dismayed reaction to American cancellation of the Skybolt
project in 1962.

discord as harmony into the Anglo-American relationship. The risk has been recently illustrated by the decoupling of U.S. and U.K. policies on nuclear testing.

In 1979, the Thatcher government inherited from its Labour predecessor the commitment to work toward a Comprehensive Test Ban Treaty. Though not repudiating this as an ultimate goal, successive Conservative administrations through the 1980s were clearly in no hurry to advance its realization. On this policy they found themselves in harmony with the Reagan and Bush administrations; and the reaction in London was no more enthusiastic than that in the White House when, in October 1992, the Congress legislated for a nine-month moratorium on nuclear testing to be followed, after a three-year resumption constrained to safety-related testing, by a final end to testing as of September 1996. Echoing President Bush, a British Government spokesman termed the congressional move "unfortunate and misguided."[11]

As the rather different views of first candidate, and subsequently president-elect, Clinton became apparent, London muted its opposition; but it conspicuously failed to join Washington, Paris, and Moscow in declaring a formal moratorium, even though the British were in practice debarred from testing at the Nevada Test Site by the U.S. suspension. U.K. Government statements made plain a skepticism about how far a test ban would in practice curb nuclear proliferation (bearing in mind that, of the assumed successful proliferants to date--Israel, India, South Africa, Pakistan, and perhaps North Korea--only the Indians are known to have conducted a test) and drew attention to the safety case for some level of continued testing (the argument of responsible nuclear ownership).[12]

---

[11]House of Lords Official Report, October 1992, col. 447.

[12]See, for example, Prime Minister Major responding to parliamentary questions from Paul Flynn, M.P.: "A comprehensive test ban would not in itself prevent a proliferator from producing and deploying a crude nuclear weapon without recourse to testing, and from obtaining the materials with which to do this. . . ."; and "The factors which will influence the rate at which progress towards a ban can be made will include the need to develop an effective system of verification. We will also need to be confident that we have the necessary technologies and expertise to maintain the safety of our

Despite the clear policy divergence, the issue never came close to constituting a row between Washington and London. As its policy took shape, the U.S. administration was punctilious about consulting U.K. interests, while making it clear that these could not be the determinant. The United Kingdom was punctilious in acknowledging that it tested at Nevada only by courtesy of the United States and in avoiding interference in the debate in the United States. The Administration's eventual decision to roll forward the moratorium[13] was undoubtedly a disappointment to the United Kingdom, but the matter had been handled on both sides so as to avoid rancor. In his King's College, London, speech of November 1993, British Defence Secretary Rifkind was able to affirm that the United Kingdom was "ready to participate fully and constructively in negotiations to secure a comprehensive test ban"--even while noting with British understatement that "this has not been an entirely easy decision for us." But the fact that, over this specific issue, transatlantic ructions had been avoided did not alter the situation that a question of nuclear policy had become an occasion of difference rather than convergence between the two countries.

This would matter less if the overall relationship between Washington and London were in better shape. Regrettably, it is not. This situation reflects factors partly specific to the current interactions between the two capitals and partly to a long-term trend. For much of the post-1945 period, the instinct of U.S. national security policymakers has been to view Britain, and Washington's historically close relationship with London, as wasting assets. Britain has been perceived as a postimperial power in decline that has chosen to marginalize itself in Europe. Successive administrations have come to office with the intention of investing more heavily in their relationships with Bonn and Paris, the power centers of the more closely

---

nuclear weapons at the highest level without testing." House of Commons Official Report, March 22, 1993, col. 467.

[13]Initially, to September 1994, as announced by President Clinton in his radio address on July 3, 1993. Subsequently extended to September 1995 (see "Clinton extends Moratorium on Nuclear Tests until 1995," *International Herald Tribune*, March 16, 1994, p. 5).

integrated Europe which from the U.S. has seemed geostrategically desirable, historically inevitable, and administratively tidy.

In office, the assessment has tended to change. Paris in particular has proved remarkably tenacious of national interests not consonant with those of the United States. European cohesion has often turned out to mean a reluctance to admit U.S. arguments or influence until an unalterable common European position has been hammered out, of a kind (as, for example, in the GATT) not necessarily welcome to the United States. Britain's readiness to accommodate U.S. views and its own self-appointed role as promoter of transatlantic harmony have come to seem more attractive traits as each new administration's focus has narrowed under the pressure of events from geostrategic theorizing to day-to-day problem-solving. And Britain's stock has also usually recovered when her willingness is demonstrated anew to share the risks of Western military intervention (whether in Beirut, in the bombing of Tripoli, or in the Gulf).

There is, however, little sign so far of this cycle of British rehabilitation in Washington's eyes repeating itself under the Clinton administration. The personal chemistry in key positions is not good. Bosnia, the sort of contingency that in years past might have proved a bonding experience between London and Washington, has so far proved only a source of friction. The admission of Sinn Fein's Gerry Adams to the United States, a reversal of the long-standing policy of previous administrations, was both a powerful symbol of, and perhaps a contributing factor to, deterioration of the bilateral relationship. And, perhaps in consequence of a new focus on the Pacific Rim, the administration's preference for viewing Europe as a whole remains intact--as out-going U.S. Ambassador to London Raymond Seitz reminded his audience in his valedictory address: "America's transatlantic policy is European in scope. . . . It is the policy of one continent to another."[14] For Britain, he suggested, the path to influence in Washington must now lie through Paris and Bonn.

---

[14]"U.S. Ambassador Leaves with Rebuke for Euro-sceptics," *London Times*, April 20, 1994, p. 1.

Taken together, the divergence of nuclear attitudes and the weakened state of broader Anglo-American relations imply the risk that nuclear affairs, once a key link between Washington and London, could come to represent just a further irritant in a diminished relationship. If this situation is to be avoided, and if nuclear cooperation is to continue on the same basis of mutual confidence and benefit as in the past, then it will be helpful if evolving British and U.S. views about the role of nuclear weapons--and in particular the U.K. deterrent--in international security remain if not identical then at least compatible. Put another way, it will be important for the United States to continue to regard the United Kingdom's independent nuclear deterrent as, on balance, a net asset to international security.

The requirement, then, is for a redefined rationale for the U.K. deterrent that demonstrates its relevance to British, and, more broadly, Western security interests; that conduces to harmony rather than discord between Britain and her principal friends and allies, notably the United States; which is intellectually coherent; and that reflects the altered reality of the post-Cold War world. The following three sections examine three leading candidates for such a redefined rationale: (1) as a "catalyst for denuclearization;" (2) as a deterrent to new threats from proliferation; and (3) as a building-block of European Union.

4. A CATALYST FOR DENUCLEARIZATION?

"Nothing in his life became him like the leaving it"--Malcolm's obituary[1] on the Thane of Cawdor suggests one possible role model for the British nuclear deterrent. If, in the transformed world, the point and purpose of that deterrent is no longer obvious, then surely the right policy, it may be argued, is to give it up. The moral and political leverage that would accrue from voluntary nuclear disarmament would provide powerful support to those policies of denuclearization and nonproliferation that (again, it may be argued) should now represent the top security priorities of the Western democracies.

True, total abolition of the U.K. deterrent does not look on the political cards in any reasonably foreseeable timescale. As we noted in Section 1 there is now consensus among the main U.K. political parties on the need to retain nuclear weapons, at least "as long as other countries possess them." But a commitment of this kind could still be satisfied at very much lower levels of armament than those now current or planned. There is a great deal of nuclear divestment which could take place short of total elimination--and which, by this analysis, might itself serve to promote the conditions in which final renunciation of U.K. nuclear weapons would at last be possible.

PLANNED U.K. NUCLEAR REDUCTIONS

At this point, account must briefly be taken of the extent to which reductions in the U.K.'s nuclear capabilities are already scheduled, following a series of decisions taken by the British government since 1991. To set these in context, the preexistent status of Britain's nuclear forces, actual and planned, must first be outlined.

As the Cold War ended, Britain's nuclear capability consisted of an aging four-boat submarine force deploying the U.S. Polaris ballistic missile system and a stockpile of similarly aging nuclear gravity bombs--the WE177 weapon--primarily intended for delivery against land targets by Tornado fighter-bombers (11 squadrons of these dual-capable

---

[1]William Shakespeare, *Macbeth*, 1.4.7.

aircraft were available). In addition, two squadrons of Royal Air Force
(RAF) Buccaneers were assigned for nuclear strike against surface ships,
while the Royal Navy's (RN) Sea Harriers could deliver the WE177 against
land or sea-to-surface targets and RN helicopters could deploy the same
weapon as a depth bomb against submarines. Several British systems were
also assigned to deliver U.S. nuclear warheads under NATO "dual key"
arrangements; these comprised a regiment of Lance missiles and a battery
of 155-millimeter howitzers based in Germany and the RAF's Nimrod
maritime patrol aircraft (in their antisubmarine role).

The Polaris submarine force had entered service beginning in 1968.
As we noted above, the long lead time required by a replacement prompted
the decision as early as 1980 to replace the four-boat Polaris force
with a four-boat Trident force in the 1990s. The economic advantages of
maintaining commonality with U.S. systems then dictated the selection of
the D5 Trident missile, with its technical capability to lift 12
warheads; as what might be termed a self-denying ordnance, the British
government announced in 1982 that it would deploy no more than 8 (the
number associated with the C4 version of the Trident missile). Even so,
it seemed on this basis that the U.K. Trident could represent a
significant increase in firepower over Polaris--up to 8 warheads per
missile as opposed to the evident maximum of 3 on Polaris. Critics
would multiply these figures by 16 for the missile-tubes per boat and by
4 for the boats per force, to assert that the government was planning to
increase its strategic nuclear capability from an assumed 192 warheads
for the Polaris force to an assumed 512 with Trident. Declining to
specify numbers, the government nonetheless acknowledged the potential
increase in capability and defended it by reference to the Soviet
Union's advances in antiballistic missile defense.

As for the WE177, the government made plain that it was looking to
replace it around the turn of the century or some time thereafter (the
date receded over time), with an air-to-surface missile that would allow
strike aircraft to stand off the increasingly capable Warsaw-Pact air
defenses. Two American systems were under study along with the
possibility of a collaborative project with France (the Air-Sol Longue
Portée, or ASLP).

Such, then, was the position as Warsaw Pact and Soviet Union unravelled--prompting a series of nuclear divestment decisions that point the way to significantly smaller British nuclear forces, even when Trident is fully in service. The process began with the decision by NATO defense ministers in October 1991 to scrap the Alliance's nuclear tube artillery and Lance missiles and to substantially reduce the remaining stockpile of gravity bombs. This decision had been anticipated the previous month by President Bush's announcement[2] of his intention to abolish these short-range ground-launched nuclear systems and to withdraw all maritime tactical nuclear weapons from the U.S. fleet "under normal circumstances." London immediately followed Washington's lead on the withdrawal of maritime weapons and the following June, went further than any of the other nuclear-weapon states by announcing the decision to eliminate this capability entirely (that is, to scrap all nuclear depth bombs, to abandon the Buccaneer's maritime strike role, and to give up the Sea Harrier's nuclear capability).[3]

Meanwhile, the number of nuclear-capable Tornado squadrons was reducing from eleven to eight; and, in parallel with the NATO decision to reduce its gravity bomb holdings, the British defence secretary announced the halving of the WE177 stockpile. Uncertainty gathered over the future of the air-to-surface missile project, until finally, in October 1993, Defence Secretary Rifkind announced the decision not to proceed.[4] The matter would be kept under review; and national capability to design, develop, and produce nuclear weapons would be safeguarded. But, barring new circumstances forcing a change of plan, the prospect was that, once the residual WE177 stockpile reached the end of its service life in the first decade of the new century, British nuclear capability would be vested solely in the new Trident force.

---

[2]In his television address of September 27, 1991--see *Weekly Compilation of Presidential Documents* of September 30, 1991.
[3]House of Commons Official Report, June 15, 1992, col. 422.
[4]House of Commons Official Report, October 18, 1993, col. 34.

Finally, to complete the nuclear houseclearing, Malcolm Rifkind announced the following month[5] a further reduction of the upper limit of warheads to be deployed with the Trident force, to a maximum of 96 per boat. (This figure implies an average of up to six per missile, but allows scope for variation in the loading of individual missiles--a flexibility that might well be desirable once the gravity-bomb option is no longer available.) Rifkind noted that "when Trident is fully in service the explosive power of the United Kingdom's operational nuclear inventory, comprising both strategic and substrategic systems, will be more than 25 percent down on the 1990 figure." The final retirement of the remaining WE177 stockpile will push this lower yet.

None of this, however, should be mistaken for a Pauline conversion of the Conservative government to the cause of unilateral nuclear disarmament. A mix of motives may be supposed. In some cases resource constraints weighed heavily (and were explicitly acknowledged as a decisive factor in relation to the aborted air-to-surface missile project).[6] In others, a genuine attachment to "minimum deterrence"--the long-standing commitment of successive British governments to avoid unnecessary redundancy in the arsenal--seems to have been the determinant; it was certainly cited in explanation of the decision to abolish the maritime tactical nuclear capability.[7] And in all cases the government will have been well aware of the value of judicious and progressive nuclear reductions in disarming its critics, whether domestic or overseas.[8]

---

[5]Speech at Centre for Defence Studies, King's College, London, November 16, 1993; hereafter "King's College speech."

[6]". . . we have concluded that our previous requirement for a new standoff nuclear weapon capability is not a sufficiently high priority to justify the procurement of a new nuclear system in the current circumstances." Malcolm Rifkind, House of Commons Official Report, October 18, 1993, col. 34.

[7]"The Government are committed to maintaining the United Kingdom's nuclear arsenal at the minimum level necessary for our deterrent needs." Malcolm Rifkind, House of Commons Official Report, June 15, 1992, announcing the ending of the U.K.'s maritime tactical nuclear weapon capability.

[8]At home, consensus at Westminster on the need to retain a deterrent did not, of course, preclude continuing disagreement about its appropriate size and shape; and both Labour and Liberal-Democrat

Far, then, from embracing the unilateralist's agenda, the Conservative government was in fact cleaving to the 1991 NATO new Strategic Concept--demonstrating a "reduced reliance" on nuclear weapons while at the same time holding tight to a conviction of their continuing essentiality to the maintenance of peace in Europe. Malcolm Rifkind spelled it out again in his King's College speech: "The value of nuclear weapons in such circumstances lies . . . in actually preventing war. NATO has always seen nuclear weapons in these terms, as part of an integrated approach to war prevention. The proposition is embodied again in NATO's new Strategic Concept, and I remain utterly convinced of its validity." Going on to reject "no first use" declarations, Rifkind is in short enunciating the classic Blessing in Disguise view described in the previous section.

By contrast, the "catalyst for denuclearization" strategy would embody a fundamentally Ultimate Evil attitude to the British deterrent. It would view that deterrent as primarily a source of moral and political capital to be expended in whatever ways might best promote the capping, reduction, and elimination of nuclear arsenals worldwide. The consignment of the capability to formal disarmament talks might be one way; further reductions presented and intended to serve as an example to others could be another.

Historically, the adoption of a policy approach that gave primacy to disarmament over preservation of Britain's position as a nuclear-weapon state would have been open to the objections of damaging Britain's relations with the United States and undermining her international standing. It may be doubted how much force would attach to either objection today. The new U.S. attitudes to nuclear weapons and their place in international affairs suggest that Washington would hardly object were London to make clear that it was ready to set course

---

spokesmen continued to criticize the government for the increase in the number of strategic warheads that even the new limit of 96 per Trident boat would represent. Abroad, there were still many ready to suggest that Britain was not living up to its disarmament commitments in the NPT context and/or that it was time for the U.K. deterrent to be brought within a formal arms control process.

for the ultimate abolition of the U.K. deterrent, in the pursuit of nonproliferation and denuclearization.

Nor does the "international standing" argument cut much ice these days. Most Britons have become accustomed to think of their country as a middle-ranking power amongst others and to reflect that Britain's future strategic status, to the extent that it matters at all, will be much less dependent on nuclear weapons than on the country's will and ability to participate in such operations as the liberation of Kuwait. If there has been skepticism in London over U.S. proposals to expand the membership of the UN Security Council to include Germany and Japan, this has had more to do with concerns about how the process of expansion once begun could be limited, and with doubts about whether either country is yet ready and willing to assume broad international security resonsibilities, than with any desire to maintain the current congruity between the Security Council's permanent membership and the recognized nuclear-weapon states.

Indeed, a Britain that sought out a leading international role in the promotion of nuclear disarmament and that made clear that it saw the primary purpose and responsibility of its nuclear status as the advancement of denuclearization and nonproliferation could arguably lay claim to an enhanced international moral authority. It would certainly find itself working much more nearly with the current international grain. Yet, if the historical objections to such a change of posture have largely lost their force, three others remain which deserve scrutiny: that such a policy would undermine NATO; that it would be ineffective; and that it could, indeed, be counterproductive. These objections are considered in turn below.

WOULD A "CATALYST" POLICY UNDERMINE NATO?

To answer first a different question, it would certainly undermine NATO's new Strategic Concept. As we have seen, though endorsing "reduced reliance," the Concept embodies essentially the Blessing in Disguise view of nuclear weapons. Were one of the two Alliance nations who assign nuclear forces to NATO to adopt policies--and in particular to adopt a "no first use" policy--reflecting an Ultimate Evil view of nuclear weapons, the Strategic Concept would have to be revised.

In parallel and in consequence, such a British policy shift could also be expected to encourage the demise of the current NATO arrangements for "risk- and burden-sharing" between the nuclear and nonnuclear allies. European allies currently cooperate with the United States in such matters as the provision of storage facilities (under U.S. custody) for U.S. nuclear weapons; the basing of U.S. strike aircraft; and the assignment of national dual-capable aircraft ready to deliver U.S. nuclear bombs in time of war.

Beyond the demonstration of allied solidarity and commitment to a common purpose, these arrangements have fostered Alliance cohesion by admitting nonnuclear allies to NATO's inner nuclear counsels through participation in the ministerial Nuclear Planning Group (NPG).[9] Apart from providing a valuable Alliance forum for coordination on the major nuclear decisions,[10] the NPG, like the High Level Group of officials that services it, has also served a powerful institutional purpose. By virtue of the very fact of its existence and activity, it has created, in each of the individual member nations, a constituency for the collective nuclear policy.

The key point, however, about the "burden-sharing" arrangements has been to reinforce deterrence. Nuclear forces actually based in Europe, with wide participation by European allies, have embodied the possibility of nuclear response to an overwhelming conventional attack on NATO Europe--the more credible in that their use could be envisaged in ways that would not inevitably mean escalation to the sort of intercontinental exchanges that would threaten destruction of the U.S. homeland. It is this that the NATO Strategic Concept has in mind when it notes that "nuclear forces based in Europe . . . provide an essential

---

[9]Founded in 1967 (with a remit to work out the nuclear elements of the newly embraced strategy of Flexible Response), this group of defense ministers has met twice a year ever since, until latterly alternating between Brussels and "hosted" meetings in one or another of the member nations' countries.

[10]For example, the "twin-track" decision of 1979 that led to the deployment of Cruise and Pershing missiles in Europe and the 1991 decision to cut the nuclear stockpile in Europe.

political and military link between the European and North American members of the Alliance." The connection between the European basing of nuclear forces and NATO's reservation of the right to make first use of nuclear weapons in self-defense was accurately pointed up by Les Aspin in his 1992 paper.[11] Arguing the need to reconsider the policy of first use "which may, if it remains intact, undercut our nonproliferation efforts by legitimizing nuclear weapons and nuclear use," he noted that "Tactical nuclear weapons have always been aimed at making our threat of nuclear first use more credible. . . . In close consultation with our NATO Allies, we now need to reconsider the possibility of withdrawing and later eliminating remaining air delivered tactical nuclear weapons in Europe."

This analysis suggests that the adoption of an overarching "catalyst for denuclearization" policy for the U.K. deterrent would, if successfully translated to the wider Alliance, mean the end of current NATO strategy, of the basing of U.S. nuclear forces in Europe, and of an important institutional element of Alliance solidarity. But what of it? Surely, it can be argued, are these developments now not improbable, anyway, irrespective of British policy? Nor, in the post-Cold War world, need they be viewed as unhealthy. Both these points need consideration before a judgment may be reached on the "undermining NATO" objection.

Certainly, the relegation of nuclear affairs in NATO's preoccupations over the past two or three years is a matter of observable fact. The NPG is a useful indicator--and the institution is now plainly running out of steam. The hosted meeting at Gleneagles in Scotland in the fall of 1992 seems likely to be the last away from Brussels. It has become increasingly hard to discern a useful agenda for either NPG or HLG. With the disappearance of the threat to the East, the heart and heat has gone out of intra-Alliance discussion of the traditional issues of deterrence. It was symptomatic that whereas it took the NPG the first 19 years of its existence to formulate and agree the General Political Guidelines on nuclear use which elaborated

---

[11]Op. cit.

the nuclear aspects of Flexible Response, the process of revising them
to conform with NATO's new Strategic Concept of 1991 and to produce a
new set of "Political Principles" on the same theme was evidently
accomplished in less than a year.[12] No one much cares any more.

The conditions described above render NATO's residual force posture
in Europe increasingly precarious. There may be a general reluctance to
see the question of the size[13] of the remaining stockpile reopened soon.
Nations would hesitate, too, to be the first to signify an unwillingness
to see U.S. nuclear weapons any longer retained on their soil. But no
such respect will be paid to the aspects of force posture that
complement the stockpile size (notably numbers of dual-capable aircraft
and main operating bases). Already, since the Alliance determination of
the new stockpile figure, this infrastructure has been eroded. To close
one of its strike bases in the U.K., these aspects, though less
talismanic than weapon numbers, are nonetheless important to the
maintenance of a credible force posture--"credible" not just to
potential adversaries but also to those within the NATO nations who
must, if the arrangements are to survive, continue to persuade
themselves and others that the exercise has enduring value. If faith in
the enterprise ebbs, so too will the readiness to fund, e.g., the
expensive custodial arrangements in the face of competing demands on
constrained defense budgets. The infrastructure (operating bases and
storage sites) can be expected to contract further, the key question
being whether the process will stop short of a complete opt-out by any
individual nation. Were that to happen, the unraveling of the whole
system would be rapid.

---

[12]The new Strategic Concept was agreed at the NATO Summit on
November 7, 1991. *The Communiqué of the NPG meeting at Gleneagles*,
released on October 21, 1992, notes allusively that ". . . we
further refined policy guidance in accordance with our new Strategic
Concept. . . ." It was left to German Defense Minister Rühe, at his
subsequent press conference, to identify this "guidance" as the
replacement for the old General Political Guidelines.

[13]Public reports suggest (see "NATO Will Cut Atom Weapons for
Aircraft Use," *New York Times*, October 18, 1991, p. A1) that, following
the 80 percent cuts agreed by the NATO defense ministers in October
1991, only a few hundred U.S. free-fall bombs are left in Europe.

Arguably, this is only a matter of time, anyway. As we have seen, the British have announced that they do not plan a replacement for the aging WE177 bomb when it is withdrawn from service in the first decade of the next century. The U.S. B61 is a younger weapon. But it, too, cannot be made to last indefinitely; and, barring some dramatic change in international circumstances, modernization of its capability looks highly unlikely.[14] The prospect is that NATO's land-based nuclear capability in Europe will simply wither on the vine. In such circumstances, as the experience with Lance in the late 1980s demonstrated, it becomes increasingly hard for defenders of a system to sustain the case for its retention when its days are numbered, anyway.[15]

On this analysis it is hard to see how--absent a significant change in international circumstances--a combination of financial pressures, "loss of faith," and advancing obsolescence will not in due course bring about the end of the U.S.-stationed nuclear presence in Europe. This could occur either by mutual agreement or by one early defection from the burden-sharing arrangements, providing the other nonnuclear-weapon states with the opportunity to express an unwillingness to be "singularized" and, hence, to follow suit. A significant effort of U.S. leadership would be required to avert such a situation: but what with budgetary pressures, the general disposition to "de-emphasize" the nuclear in security affairs, and earlier breaching of the old "no nukes, no troops" principle in Korea, such an effort seems in current circumstances (to repeat this important caveat) highly unlikely.

---

[14]This judgment is based upon European (particularly German) reluctance to contemplate accepting a tactical air-to-surface missile (TASM) on their territory, in the days before the Bush Administration cancelled the project, as well as the more general opacity surrounding the replacement of current U.S. nuclear systems in a post-Test Ban world.

[15]The argument they have to confront is that, if there is no future requirement for the capability, how much less can it be needed in the near term, when a discernible threat is almost entirely absent? Surely the savings from its retirement should be taken now. (The counterargument that the lack of a future requirement is not a given, but only a planning assumption which events may well confound, may be logically impeccable but lacks persuasive force.)

An end to the U.S. peacetime nuclear presence in Europe would not inevitably mean abandoning NATO's current strategy and nuclear policy. Flexible Response could arguably survive what might be viewed as simply a further relaxation of Alliance force posture. U.S. nuclear forces and weapons could be repatriated on the basis that a combination of increased warning time and financial pressures made this the most logical course: dual-basing of U.S. strike aircraft and redeployment of weapons in time of tension might remain part of the official doctrine. Alternatively, and especially if withdrawn weapons were actually destroyed (as life-expired or simply redundant), it could be argued that NATO's doctrine of limited, initial use could as well be carried out by offshore, or even intercontinental, systems as by weapons based in Europe; the U.K. decision to designate its Trident system for the sub-strategic (i.e., limited strike) role could be adduced as precedent.

It would not, however, be easy to manage such a significant change in NATO's nuclear force posture without precipitating fundamental strategy change at the same time. We have already noted that a principal purpose of the stationing of nuclear forces in Europe has been to make the nuclear option under Flexible Response more plausible; there would be a strong temptation to argue that the end of the one should imply the end of the other. And it is probably in this regard that the adoption by Britain of a "catalyst for denuclearization" policy with regard to its own deterrent forces would impact most significantly on the Alliance--that is, by tending to ensure that force posture changes driven primarily by budget constraints were accompanied by fundamental changes to established Alliance strategy and policy.

Would this matter? The question needs viewing from two perspectives, those of internal cohesion and external security. Internal cohesion is particularly important to an Alliance the value of which, historically, has lain as much in preventing the European powers from falling out amongst themselves as in providing a collective security against external threat. The nations of Western Europe may one day arrive at the point where they have fully sublimated ancient national rivalries in the "ever closer union among the peoples of Europe" which the Maastricht Treaty presages. But, for the moment, a

vigorous North Atlantic Alliance, with continued close U.S. involvement
in European security affairs, seems indispensable. No doubt, in the
wake of the Cold War, a more balanced partnership between the European
and North American wings of the Alliance is both desirable and
necessary. But stability requires a continuing leadership role by the
United States, as the preeminent power of the Alliance's (currently) 16
member states.[16]

Heretofore, the nuclear component of Alliance strategy has been
fundamental both to Alliance cohesion and to U.S. primacy. But it would
be wrong to infer from the premise that cohesion and U.S. primacy remain
highly important, that the nuclear component must therefore remain
fundamental. On the contrary, if NATO is to have a future, it is clear
that it must find its salvation elsewhere. As the slogan "out of area
or out of business"[17] suggests, if the Alliance is to survive, it needs
a new mission, or at least a new sense of mission. However this
evolves--whether by enlargement of the Alliance's membership, by
Partnerships for Peace or other means of "projecting stability" to the
East (or South), by increased involvement in international peacekeeping
tasks, or by some other route--U.S. leadership seems indispensable.
Only the United States has the economic and political weight, the
military resources (particularly logistic depth, capability for
strategic lift, and intelligence and communications assets), and,
perhaps, the political will that will be needed if the Alliance is to
succeed in a new post-Cold War role. But nuclear issues and nuclear
capabilities seem unlikely to play anything other than a peripheral part
in this process of Alliance evolution. Continuation of nuclear

---

[16] More than 30 years ago, Albert Wohlstetter--(see "Nuclear
Sharing: NATO and the N + 1 Country," *Foreign Affairs,* April 1961)
noted that there was "little enthusiasm for an English SACEUR (Supreme
Allied Commander, Europe) in France, for a German SACEUR in England, for
a Turkish SACEUR . . . and so on." The situation is little different
today; and the choice of the first non-American SACEUR would be only the
most obvious of the many and potentially self-generating problems that
would arise if the United States ceased to be the clear *primus inter
pares* within the Alliance.

[17]For an influential exposition of this thesis, see Ronald D.
Asmus, Richard L. Kugler, and F. Stephen Larrabee, "Building a New
NATO," *Foreign Affairs*, September/October 1993.

"business as usual" (European basing of nuclear forces, risk- and burden-sharing arrangements--even current doctrine on nuclear use) is neither a necessary nor a sufficient condition for the survival of the Alliance.

All that said, the further question remains: would the external security of the NATO allies be prejudiced by the sort of strategy and policy changes which a U.K. "catalyst of denuclearization" policy might well precipitate? If stationed nuclear forces were withdrawn, and the alliance made it plain that it would henceforward meet any aggression short of nuclear attack solely with its conventional forces, would anything be lost? Who is going, in the foreseeable future, to threaten the territory of any of the fourteen NATO European nations in ways to which the nuclear deterrent threat could be remotely relevant? The threat of overwhelming invasion from the East has evaporated. Russia is safely behind the reverse glacis that the countries of Central and Eastern Europe have now become. The foreseeable future threats to NATO Europe seem likely to be either undeterrable (such as spillover of ethnic conflict), or of a kind which the Alliance could handle with ease with the conventional forces at its disposal. To the extent that Russia's strategic nuclear arsenal remained a threat, then the U.S. strategic arsenal would continue to counterbalance it. Besides, the NATO nations now describe Russia as a partner, not an adversary.

The contrary view would argue for retention of the fundamentals of NATO's current strategy--Flexible Response, and in particular the reservation of the right to make first use of nuclear weapons in self-defense--essentially as a form of insurance. As Sir Michael Quinlan has pointed out, "military security provision is in the business of insuring against disagreeable outcomes, not preferred or even likeliest ones."[18] It would not seem unduly pessimistic to believe that challenges to peace and security in Western Europe are only in remission, not eradicated for all time. Immediate threats may have lifted; but risks remain.

---

[18]"British Nuclear Weapons Policy: Past, Present and Future," in John C. Hopkins and Weixing Hu, eds., *Strategic Views from the Second Tier: The Nuclear Weapons Policies of France, Britain, and China*, San Diego: Institute on Global Conflict and Cooperation, University of California, 1994.

The most obvious threat is that of a recidivist Russia. The Russian threat is as much an issue of politics as of military capabilities. Of course, the West needs to be aware of the vast overhang of nuclear weapons in the former Soviet Union, redundant after the START treaties, but requiring at least a decade and probably much longer to dismantle. It must similarly recall the huge military forces of all kinds that Russia can be expected to possess for the foreseeable future, even when all the various reductions are made. Mainly, however, the West needs to concern itself with the evidence that autocracy and imperialism are clearly far from vanquished in Russia and consider what strategies can best be relied upon to counter such tendencies. True, the time when a neo-imperialist Russia could again threaten Western Europe may seem a long way off. But "long" is always the relevant timescale in considering nuclear provision, given the extended lead times required to generate the capabilities involved. And it is even arguable that a Western Alliance that unemphatically but unambiguously kept its guard up might diminish the appeal in Russian eyes of the adventurism advocated by Vladimir Zhirinovsky and his allies.

Beyond that, retention of the existing strategic framework in Europe might seem advisable simply on the basis of insurance against the unforeseen. Some Middle Eastern proliferator, for example, equipped with weapons of mass destruction and long-range delivery means, might well come to threaten at least the countries of the southern flank. Of course, questions arise about the relevance of nuclear deterrence in such circumstances (which are considered in more detail in the next section); but it would certainly seem unwise to conclude that NATO's nuclear capability could have no role to play in protection of the Alliance from threats such as these. Further ahead, the possibilities multiply. The fact that no massive totalitarian threat has yet emerged to succeed that of Soviet power in the way that the Soviet threat succeeded that of Nazism seems an inadequate assurance against its possible future materialization--just as the fact that the source of such a threat cannot be identified with certainty in advance is a poor reason for denying the possibility of its occurrence.

Such considerations suggest that, other things being equal, NATO (and the U.K.) might do well to err on the side of caution before changing policies and doctrines that have served well for so many years. But *are* other things equal? Does policy conservatism in this area mean foregoing potentially greater countervailing gains? Might not the adoption by the United Kingdom of a "catalyst for denuclearization" policy for its nuclear deterrent contribute to the elimination at source of just those risks and potential future threats we have been discussing? It is to this question--whether the gains that could flow from such a policy might outweigh the potential dangers involved--that we must now turn.

WOULD A "CATALYST" POLICY BE EFFECTIVE?

What gains for international security might be hoped for from the adoption of such a policy? And how might they be secured? Taking the overarching objective to be progress towards the ultimate abolition of nuclear weapons, the aim must presumably be to find a way in which reduction or other circumscription of the United Kingdom's nuclear deterrent capability would elicit matching moves by some or all of the other four recognized nuclear-weapon states--and/or which would inhibit or even roll back nuclear proliferation elsewhere.

Yet, exactly how the United Kingdom could "cash in its nuclear chips" in this way is not obvious. One option might be to seek involvement in any new round of nuclear arms control talks between the United States and Russia. The issue here is whether such U.K. involvement would help more than it would hinder. The result might depend on just how deep any further superpower arsenal cuts were intended to be. It is, for example, sometimes suggested that the United States and Russia should press on to a "START III" agreement to reduce their strategic arsenals to as little as a few hundred warheads each. Were reductions on that scale under serious consideration, it seems inevitable that the Russians would insist on British, French, and Chinese weapons being brought into the calculation and constrained in parallel. In such circumstances, a British readiness to enter arms control negotiations and accept verified cutbacks could be very important.

But such a scenario currently seems highly improbable. When even START I remains unratified by Moscow (pending Ukraine's accession to the NPT), and when implementation of the cuts already agreed will by the most optimistic assessments take a further decade, talk of START III seems premature. Indeed, Pentagon officials have made clear that the Nuclear Posture Review completed in September 1994 uses the START II limits as the basis of force planning into the next century.[19] Other parts of the administration might be less categoric in ruling out some further agreed downward adjustment in Russian and American arsenal sizes in due course. But, in any such exercise short of the radical cuts discussed above, the introduction of third-party holdings into the calculus would probably be an unwelcome complication. Indeed, one of the preconditions of the success so far of strategic arms control has been that it has been conducted on the basis of parity between the two nuclear superpowers, with third-country systems, at U.S. insistence, excluded from what has been a strictly bilateral process. The replacement of bilateral with multiparty negotiations would remove this accepted premise of bilateral parity, as well as adding enormously to the complexity of the process.[20] If the United Kingdom has nuclear assets that it is ready to get rid of, it might seem more sensible that it should get on with doing so, rather than hang on to them in the hopes of trading them in some future negotiation that would stand a better chance of success without U.K. involvement.

---

[19]See "Uncertainty over Russia Clouds U.S. Nuclear Review," *Defense News*, June 20–26, 1994, p. 38. Assistant Secretary of Defense Harold Smith is quoted thus: "We do not expect to go below START II--after all, that is going out to the 21st century. The government of the United States can address those questions at some later date."

[20]For an illustration of the daunting complexities potentially involved in a multiparty strategic arms reduction arrangement, see Alexei G. Arbatov, "Multilateral Nuclear Weapons Reductions and Limitations," in John C. Hopkins and Weixing Hu, eds., *Strategic Views from the Second Tier: The Nuclear Weapons Policies of France, Britain, and China*, San Diego: Institute on Global Conflict and Cooperation, University of California, 1994.

Nor does it seem any more likely that the United Kingdom could succeed in negotiating concessions from clandestine proliferators in exchange for further reducing or even eliminating its own nuclear capability. The very fact that it suits both proliferators and the international community to maintain the fiction of only five recognized nuclear-weapon states (despite its being an open secret that at least Israel, India, and Pakistan now have nuclear weapons) limits the scope for a formal arms control approach. It would, of course, be desirable to see these countries eventually give up their arsenals and accede to the NPT. But the idea that they might be induced to do so by U.K. undertakings to reduce or eliminate its own nuclear capability seems implausible, while any suggestion that North Korea or Iran might be similarly induced to abandon their nuclear ambitions seems less probable still.

But this may be to take too mechanistic a view. Some formal "quid pro quo" trade-off might be less important than the straightforward setting of an example aimed at consolidating a climate of opinion against the use of nuclear threats in international affairs. The most effective way for the nuclear possessors to reduce the saliency of nuclear weapons might be to demonstrate that they no longer attach the importance to their own deterrent capabilities that they once did and that they are ready to see those capabilities reduced, constrained, and ultimately even eliminated. It is in this sort of context that a declaration of "no first use" makes sense. From an unsympathetic perspective, such declarations might seem vacuous. No one believed the Soviet "no first use" pledge that was formally in force from 1982 until its cancellation in the new draft Russian military doctrine of 1993.[21] Yet, it might be argued, a "no first use" declaration--and indeed the adoption of other policies urged by the "non-aligned" in the NPT context, such as a comprehensive test ban and further reductions in

---

[21]As Sir Michael Quinlan has pointed out, "No one is going to contemplate first nuclear use save in desperation. If a nuclear country is desperate, whether it be nuclear weapons or something else that has made it so, it will not let its options be narrowed by a past declaration." In "British Nuclear Weapons Policy: Past, Present and Future," in John C. Hopkins and Weixing Hu, eds., op. cit.

nuclear arsenals--could be a powerful symbol of the devaluation of nuclear weapons.

Expressed thus, the argument turns on the force of moral example in international affairs, and there is no decisive way of proving or disproving it. It may, however, be relevant to observe that in each of the four clear cases of nuclear proliferation (the three cited two paragraphs above and South Africa, which has subsequently given up its arsenal) the motive was very obviously regional.[22] In each case, the country concerned decided to incur the costs and political risks of developing a nuclear capability as a counter to perceived threats (not necessarily nuclear) posed by a neighbor or neighbors.

Of course, others (the example of Iraq springs to mind) might go after nuclear weapons with more aggressive intent: to establish regional hegemony or to put in a floor under any potential losses if military adventurism were unsuccessful. Whatever the historical record, might not states of this nature be tempted to pursue nuclear weapons at least in part by the reflection that aggressive, expansionist policies might one day bring them into collision with extraregional powers such as the Western nuclear possessors? Was not this precisely the lesson famously drawn by an Indian Army general from the Gulf War,[23] that a nation like Iraq should first acquire nuclear weapons before it confronts the United States?

One may wonder how many regional powers would in practice think it wise to base their military acquisition policies on a supposition of confrontation with one or more of the recognized nuclear-weapon states. But--to concede the point for the sake of the argument--even in these

---

[22]Four instances do not necessarily establish a general principle; but the proposition that regional motivations dominate in such decisions seems borne out by analogous proliferation processes such as that involving ballistic missiles, where the "war of the cities" between Iraq and Iran sparked a ballistic missile arms race among Middle Eastern neighbors anxious to acquire a retaliatory capability. (No one, for example, has argued that the Saudis acquired their Chinese CSS-2 missiles at this time for anything other than deterrence purposes within the region, despite their intercontinental range.)

[23]Identified as General K. Sundarji in George H. Quester and Victor A. Utgoff, "No-First-Use and Nonproliferation: Redefining Extended Deterrence," The Washington Quarterly, Spring 1994.

circumstances, would a display of "nuclear moderation" by the Western possessors have any material bearing on the proliferator's plans? This seems unlikely, for two reasons. First, because no amount of de-emphasizing of nuclear weapons can ultimately expunge the key distinction between those who have them and those who do not. No future regional tyrant, following the Indian precept, is going to be deflected by assurances by the nuclear-weapon states of restraint, or arsenal reductions, or even "virtual abolition"--none of which will alter the hard fact that possessing countries will retain a devastating military capability which others do not have. Second, even if *per impossible* more were on offer--even if the incentive to abandon proliferation were the complete and verified elimination of all the current nuclear arsenals--the disciple of the Indian logic would still need to press ahead to acquire his own nuclear weapons. For it was the *conventional* power of the United States and its coalition partners, not their nuclear capabilities, that thwarted Saddam Hussein.

These arguments suggest that it may not in practice be easy to make use of the British deterrent as a catalyst for denuclearization, either in formal arms control or by way of moral example. There is, however, a less ambitious case to be made for such a policy switch--that without a conspicuous change of tack by the recognized nuclear-weapon states the indefinite extension of the NPT, the principal international bulwark against proliferation, will be jeopardized. The Treaty's initial 25-year period expires in 1995, when the signatory states will assemble to decide "whether the Treaty shall continue in force indefinitely, or shall be extended for an additional fixed period or periods" as Article X of the NPT states and a significant bloc of "nonaligned" countries has made it plain that it is looking for substantial movement by the nuclear-weapon states in the direction of nuclear disarmament as a condition of a satisfactory outcome.

The specific issues likely to be central to the NPT extension debate are considered in more detail in Section 7. Here, it may suffice to recall that some 160 non-nuclear-weapon states (NNWS) have adhered to the NPT because they have judged that the most effective possible global nonproliferation regime is ultimately in *their* best interests. It would be a mistake to view nonproliferation as a favor done by the NNWS for the nuclear-weapon states (NWS). Indeed, it would not be the NWS that had most to lose in a world of untrammelled proliferation--countries that do not currently possess nuclear capabilities and could very well face the choice of living under the threat of intimidation or attack by nuclear-armed neighbors or of setting off down the uncertain and hugely costly road of acquiring such weapons themselves.

Thus the "non-aligned" ultimately have an interest as great as or greater than that of the NWS in the extension of the NPT. Of course, this will not prevent the NNWS from pressing the NWS on nuclear disarmament and seeking movement in that regard as the "price" of their agreement to the Treaty's extension. Nor does the fact that it would not be in their own best interests to do so provide a guarantee against their pushing this position to the point where the conference's success would be seriously jeopardized. But it does suggest that a satisfactory "price" need not be exorbitantly high or involve "concessions" by the NWS going much beyond the already significant force reductions and policy changes (including, for example, the ending by four of the five members of NWS of nuclear testing) of recent years. A successful NPT Conference outcome should be possible without the NWS feeling required to change their fundamental nuclear strategies and policies to achieve it.

COULD A "CATALYST" POLICY BE COUNTERPRODUCTIVE?

The third objection to such a policy switch is that it might be not merely ineffective but actually counterproductive--that it might result in a perverse incentive to proliferation. The argument may be most easily made at one remove, by considering the possible consequences if the United States, as the West's premier custodian of nuclear power, were to embrace a suite of Ultimate Evil policies on nuclear weapons, including a declaration of "no first use."

An interesting foretaste of where such a policy shift could lead is provided by the March/April 1994 issue of *Foreign Affairs*, which contains two separate articles dealing with the demise of U.S. extended nuclear deterrence--one arguing that "closing the nuclear umbrella" would be in America's best interests,[24] the other, that a *conventional* extended deterrent should be sought, given the "sad fact . . . that extended deterrence--the ability of the U.S. nuclear force to protect its allies--is dead."[25] Strikingly, the argument is not merely about the credibility of U.S. nuclear guarantees in the face of nonnuclear forms of aggression (where a reluctance to be the first to resort to nuclear force might be surmised even in the absence of a formal declaration); the judgment is seen as applying even in the face of nuclear-armed aggression, where "a cold-blooded despot could . . . challenge America's reluctance to legitimize nuclear force by responding in kind."

One analyst's judgment is, of course, no more than that. But the position does highlight an interesting and important point--that is, the difficulty in practice of managing a policy switch to "no first use" in a way that would not undermine U.S. allies' confidence in continued U.S. protection *even against nuclear threats.* If this undermining were to happen, then a decision to "go nuclear" by one or more of the technologically advanced states that have the ability to produce their own weapons but have so far preferred to rely on U.S. nuclear protection must be accounted rather high. Germany and Japan are usually cited in this context. Worries about the former may do less than justice to Germany's formal and repeated renunciation[26] of nuclear weapons. Some very mixed signals have, however, emanated from Japan over the past year or so, especially since the North Korean test-firing in May 1993 of a ballistic missile with the range to reach Japan.[27]

It may be asked why the Japanese should harbor doubts about the reliability of U.S. extended deterrence in the face of a North Korean

---

[24]Ted Galen Carpenter, "Closing the Nuclear Umbrella," *Foreign Affairs*, March/April 1994.

[25]Seth Cropsey, "The Only Credible Deterrent," *Foreign Affairs*, March/April 1994.

[26]Most recently in the unification treaty (properly, the "Treaty on the Final Settlement with Respect to Germany"), signed on September 12, 1990.

[27]See, for example, "In Japan, Quiet Talk of Nuclear Arms," *Boston Globe*, September 19, 1993, p. 10, or "Japan to 'Go Nuclear' in Asian Arms Race," *London Sunday Times*, January 30, 1994, p. 1.

nuclear threat when they seemingly did not do so in the face of a Soviet nuclear threat. Perhaps they simply regard the North Korean threat as more real. Or perhaps the withdrawal of U.S. nuclear forces from South Korea suggested to them something unpalatable about ultimate U.S. willingness to contemplate the use of nuclear force to defend its allies in North East Asia (we have already observed the role stationed nuclear forces play in symbolizing such willingness). Whatever the reason, it would certainly seem optimistic to argue that U.S. adoption of a "no first use" policy should be accepted with equanimity in Tokyo, on the grounds that such a move would in no way inhibit U.S. readiness to retaliate in kind to any North Korean nuclear use against Japan. Though this argument might be correct as far as it went, it would miss the wider point (as the Japanese and others very likely would not) that the prime purpose of the policy shift would be to symbolize a fundamental sea change in the U.S.'s attitude to the legitimacy and utility of nuclear weapons.

If U.S. allies might draw unhelpful conclusions from the realization of such a sea change, what of potential adversaries? Certainly, they could be expected to draw the "moral" that resort on their part to chemical or biological weapons (CBW) in any future conflict with the United States would be liable to retaliation by conventional means only. (Indeed, the whole point of a "no first use" declaration would, in a sense, be to encourage them to do so.) Since the situation would almost certainly be one in which U.S. conventional power was already heavily engaged, this could amount to making use of CBW seem a "no added cost" option. Indeed, even the nuclear option, or at least the ability to threaten it, might come to look more attractive to adversaries. Thus the Pyongyang regime, pondering U.S. initiatives to "denuclearize" the Korean peninsula, seemed--at least while Kim Il Sung was alive--less disposed to draw helpful conclusions about the diminishing role of nuclear weapons in international affairs than to interpret the policy as evidence of U.S. weakness. Observing the spectacle of a nation that had become so uncomfortable with its nuclear power that it foreswore the option of first use, it might indeed appear to any future "cold-blooded despot" that even the prospect of a second, retaliatory use could reasonably be discounted.

But how is this relevant to the U.K. deterrent? The U.K. nuclear force is assigned to NATO; but it is upon the credibility or otherwise of the U.S. nuclear umbrella that potentially nervous allies will concentrate. "Rogue" regimes, too, to the extent that extraregional considerations influence their behavior, will concern themselves with U.S., not British, attitudes and policies. These are valid points; but they ignore the scope Britain still retains, as a U.N. Security Council permanent member, as one of only five recognized nuclear-weapon states and as a depositary power of the NPT, to influence international opinion on nuclear issues--and more particularly to influence the intellectual climate within the Western Alliance and in the United States. Indeed, the most powerful direct effect that could be expected from a U.K. shift to a "catalyst for denuclearisation" rationale for its nuclear capability would be upon the development of attitudes in the United States. In this sense, such a policy shift might indeed be effective-- though whether the effect would ultimately lead to a more secure international environment is, as argued above, a very different matter.

CONCLUSION

Where has the argument taken us? The analysis suggests that the option of using the British nuclear deterrent as a "catalyst for denuclearization"--that is, of making the main aim of U.K. nuclear policy to promote disarmament and nonproliferation through progressive reductions of, and acceptance of constraints upon, the U.K. nuclear capability--has some rather serious drawbacks. Such a policy departure would have significant moral force; it would reinforce the current tide of U.S. thinking and very likely precipitate a fundamental change in NATO's nuclear policies. This might not matter. The old nuclear policies and the practical and institutional arrangements associated with them have constituted much of NATO's internal glue; but with or without policy change, such arrangements now look moribund, and the Alliance needs to recognize that it must now move on if it is to retain its cohesion and viability for the future. Yet one may accept this argument and still believe abandonment of established nuclear policy to be unwise, less for concern about the security environment of today or tomorrow than out of deference for the unknowable risks of the twenty-first century.

Such counsels of caution imply that catalyzing a reaction of nuclear policy change in the Western Alliance would be a risk worth taking only in anticipation of clear countervailing gain, in terms of disarmament or nonproliferation. But the conclusions of the analysis here are discouraging. It is hard to envisage the linkages that would allow U.K. nuclear reductions to be traded for worthwhile cutbacks elsewhere. Nor does the thesis that repudiation of nuclear force by its Western possessors would influence proliferators to change their minds seem persuasive. On the contrary, such a sea change in attitudes could result in a perverse incentive to proliferation, among friends as well as potential adversaries. On this basis, a "catalyst for denuclearization" rationale for the U.K. deterrent seems unattractive; and it is now appropriate to consider whether an altogether different concept of the relevance of the U.K. deterrent to the challenge of proliferation may not have more validity.

5.   A DETERRENT OF NEW THREATS?

The most obvious alternative rationale for the United Kingdom
deterrent in the post-Cold War world is implicit in the "new era of
peril and opportunity" described by President Clinton to the U.N.
General Assembly (see Section 2). Exit the old Soviet threat; enter the
new menace of nuclear proliferation. Or, if not new, at least
exacerbated by the risk that the disintegrative processes at work in the
former Soviet Union could result in expertise, nuclear materials, or
even weapons finding their way into the hands of those with the money to
pay for them. Many would regard it as self-evident that the primary
value of Britain's bomb is now as a counter to the ambitions of an
emerging class of "third world nuclear tyrants." The U.K. political
consensus that we noted earlier on the need for Britain to retain
nuclear weapons "as long as other countries possess them" reflects the
widespread view that the nuclear threats of the future should not be
supposed to emanate solely, or even mainly, from the successor states of
the former Soviet Union.

Yet, ministers of the present British government have shown
themselves strikingly reluctant to rededicate the U.K.'s nuclear armory
to the deterrence of new threats arising outside Europe. Speaking in
Paris in September 1992, Defence Secretary Rifkind specifically
cautioned against any "belief that nuclear deterrence is
straightforwardly exportable from the traditional East-West context."[1]
The uncertainties included how far a nuclear proliferator could be
assumed to be "susceptible . . . to the logic of deterrence as we--and
our former Soviet antagonists--have traditionally understood it;"
whether he might not be disposed to gamble on the West's being self-
deterred from use of its nuclear weapons; and how likely the United
Kingdom ever was to find itself "so deeply in conflict with a non-
European power" that nuclear deterrence could come into play in the

---

[1]"Extending Deterrence?" contribution to a colloquium on strategic
issues chaired by his French counterpart, Pierre Joxe, on September 30,
1992. Hereafter, "Paris speech."

first place. The argument stopped short of repudiation of any role for nuclear deterrence outside the traditional East-West context; but the tone was notably agnostic ("perhaps the most important conclusion is not to rush to judgment on these difficult issues: we face an evolving situation, and our analysis should continue to evolve with it").

A year later, in his King's College speech, Rifkind showed himself no readier to declare an extra-European rationale for the U.K.'s deterrent. He tied his explanation of the "positive and necessary contribution to peace and stability" made by U.K. nuclear weapons to "the context of a European contribution to the North Atlantic Alliance"--and was at pains to distinguish between this context, where a stable deterrence had evolved over long years, and other areas of the world where "it is difficult to be confident that an intended deterrent would work in the way intended, in the absence of an established nuclear deterrent relationship."

It is possible to impute an element of political calculation to this reluctance to shift ground. Any too-obvious changing of horses might just look opportunistic. And then there is the familiar need, all the more pressing as the 1995 NPT extension conference approaches, not to hand arguments to would-be proliferators. If the U.K. began to conjure new demons in justification of its continuing nuclear capabilities, then how much the more persuasively might others, geographically much closer to the demon, make the same case in defense of their acquisition of nuclear weapons? The guarding of this proliferation flank was evidently very much in Rifkind's mind in his King's College speech when he spelled out that "in contrast therefore to the situation in Europe, it is difficult to see deterrence operating securely against proliferators," and concluded that "I therefore see no contradiction between the policy for nuclear weapons I have described [their retention as a contribution to European security] and vigorous measures to prevent nuclear proliferation."

Agnosticism may be politic without being feigned. There is very evidently a real dilemma felt by all the nuclear powers as to how far, if at all, their nuclear capability can be turned to good effect in countering "rogue" states. The British defence secretary's speeches

quoted above dwell on the difficulties of transfering deterrence "rules"
to a new context, with new kinds of actors. There is also a sort of
role reversal to be taken into account, at least by the European nuclear
powers. Over the decades, the British and French have successfully
persuaded themselves that, when nuclear weapons are in play, the weak
can deter the strong--that there *is* a way in which the defending side,
though facing a nuclear superpower, could nonetheless rationally be the
first to resort to nuclear use (the "warning shot" concept), and that
overwhelming power can in the nuclear age be negated, provided that both
parties to the confrontation realize that for the weaker party what is
at stake is national survival.

Such circumstances could permit what the French term "la dissuasion
du faible au fort."[2] But, in some putative confrontation with some
future nuclear-armed Saddam Hussein, the European powers could very well
find themselves cast in the role of the "strong"--and with their
fundamental national interests perhaps less wholly engaged than those of
their antagonist. In Les Aspin's phrase, the equalizer could well find
himself the equalizee. Moreover, for the United Kingdom a further
difficulty arises from the traditional policy, described in Section 2,
of casting the British deterrent in the role of belt to the U.S.
suspenders. With ingenuity, the requirement for the belt in the
circumstances of Cold War Europe could be established; but can the belt
be represented as anything other than superfluous in the very different
situation which would obtain if, for example, a U.S.-led Western
coalition confronted a nuclear Iraq? These concerns suggest two basic
questions that would have to be answered in the affirmative before the
United Kingdom could enunciate a new rationale for its nuclear deterrent
based on new or emerging threats, namely,

- is there a role for Western nuclear deterrence outside the
  traditional East-West context? and
- even if so, is there a role in such circumstances for a
  specifically British deterrent capability?

---

[2]"Deterrence by the weak of the strong."

DETERRENCE OUTSIDE THE EAST-WEST CONTEXT

Not everyone sees this as particularly difficult. Kenneth Waltz, for example (who, as we saw earlier, favors the spread of nuclear weapons as influences for international stability) challenges what he calls the "pervasive belief . . . that nuclear deterrence is highly problematic."[3] Provided that a nuclear power does not leave its forces exposed to preemptive destruction, then "in a nuclear world any state will be deterred by another state's second-strike forces. One need not become preoccupied with the characteristics of the state that is to be deterred or scrutinize its leaders." Yet, just this sort of preoccupation and scrutinization has long been a central part of theorizing about deterrence--and seems hard to avoid in dealing with a strategy that explicitly seeks to operate on the mind of the potential aggressor. Over the years the Western nuclear powers became familiar, or so they felt, with the mind-set of the men in the Kremlin; they could be assumed to understand the capabilities of nuclear weapons and the dangers of nuclear war.[4] Fanatics and zealots in other parts of the world were something altogether different. "Deterrence," reflected Malcolm Rifkind, "depends upon the operation of a degree of rationality and caution. But what if [the antagonist] is a tyrant with little regard for the safety and welfare of his own country and people? If he is a gambler or an adventurer? If his judgment is unbalanced, or clouded by isolation?"[5] Or, as the French neatly put it, what confidence can we have in "la dissuasion du fort au fou"?[6]

The task of deterring an out-and-out madman would indeed be problematic. We may, however, incline to agree with Yehezkel Dror (the man who first gave currency to the concept of "crazy states" in his 1971 book[7] of that title) that the emergence on the international scene of a truly irrational actor is a very unlikely phenomenon. The *mores* and

---

[3]Kenneth N. Waltz, "Nuclear Myths and Political Realities," *American Political Science Review,* September 1990.

[4]On this, see for example, Lawrence Freedman, *The Evolution of Nuclear Strategy*, New York: St. Martin's Press, 1983.

[5]Paris speech.

[6]"Deterrence by the strong of the mad."

[7]Yehezkel Dror, *Crazy States: A Counterconventional Strategic Problem*, Lexington, Mass.: Heath Lexington Books, 1971.

value systems of other societies and cultures may sometimes be hard to understand--or, once understood, to regard with other than repugnance. But that is quite a different matter from irrationality. Instances where the adversary in a confrontation is impervious to the fundamental logic of deterrence--"do that and I'll make you sorry"--are likely to be very rare.

Susceptibility to deterrent logic is, however, not enough. If in any given situation a deterrent threat is reliably to influence behavior a series of other conditions must also be satisfied. The adversary must "register" the threat in such a way as to take it properly into account *before* committing himself to the course of action from which the threat is meant to deter him; he must believe that the threat can and will be implemented; and he must conclude that the loss implied by the threat would indeed outweigh the looked-for gain.

The reliability or otherwise of this process will probably depend upon how far it needs to be consciously worked through in any given situation. Fortunately, as Patrick Morgan has pointed out, it very often does not.[8] Morgan draws the distinction between what he terms "specific" or "immediate" deterrence on the one hand, and "general" deterrence on the other. The former involves a sort of conscious, threshold-of-action type of risk-calculus. It is fraught with uncertainty, something that will occur only when general deterrence has broken down or has never existed, and is mercifully rare. General deterrence, by contrast, is a preestablished mental state, a mind-set developed prior (perhaps long prior) to the specific crisis, pre-disposing the actor to reject possible particular courses of action without either needing or wanting to reexamine the issue from first principles on any specific occasion.

General deterrence was the condition eventually achieved between East and West along the Cold War's central axis of confrontation. The futility of aggression by either side became something established in the institutional culture and received wisdom of leaderships on either side. Awareness by each side of the other's secure nuclear retaliatory

---

[8]Patrick M. Morgan, *Deterrence: A Conceptual Analysis*, Sage Publications, 1977.

capability will have had much to do with this. But it is also arguable that secure "general" deterrence--in which the outcome of any specific cost/benefit assessment is largely "taken as read"--may well be dependent on the prior operation of "specific" deterrence on one or more occasions--occasions on which those to be deterred looked into the abyss, recoiled, and drew appropriate general lessons for the future.

This sort of argument seems to underlie the fundamental distinction drawn by the present British government between the secure operation of nuclear deterrence in Europe and the uncertainties about its reliability elsewhere. "Stable deterrence . . . relies crucially on a degree of mutual understanding and on the evolution or learning of a set of rules of behavior. This process of evolution or learning inevitably involves risks and opportunities for misunderstandings."[9] Secure deterrence in Europe had been achieved only after a prolonged process of "exploring where the boundaries of permissible behavior lay"--at times standing close to danger in doing so. The argument is evidently that to repeat the learning process in other contexts would be to rerun the risks of catastrophe.

The Problem Of Credibility

The concept of an established relationship of "general" deterrence suggests one reason why a policy that effectively regulated the behavior of the men in the Kremlin may be less reliable in dealing with future disruptive forces on the international scene. A second stems from the condition for successful deterrence that we noted above--that the deterrent threat should be believed. In the Cold War context, the "credibility problem" derived from the West's vulnerability to nuclear retaliation. In such circumstances, the West's threat to resort to nuclear weapons would seem plausible only in defense of the most vital of national interests.[10]

Perceptions of vulnerability should be less of a problem in establishing plausible deterrence in future confrontation with regional

---

[9]King's College speech.

[10]It was, of course, a central aim of U.S. and Alliance strategists to convince the Soviet leaders--and themselves--that the U.S. would regard aggression in Europe in just those terms.

aggressors. But there are also powerful *internal* constraints on readiness to resort to nuclear action. These constraints are sometimes discussed in terms of "Just War" theory or of international law. To the leader of a nuclear power to whom would fall the decision to authorize nuclear release (and upon whose perceived willingness to do so deterrent credibility rests), the constraints are perhaps more likely to present themselves in terms of the anticipated judgment of first his fellow countrymen and international opinion and, ultimately, of history. However they appear, their message will be essentially the same: that the action contemplated (unless in response to prior nuclear use by the other side) will breach a taboo of some 50 years' standing; that, whether intended or not, it will very probably mean the death and injury of large, perhaps very large, numbers of innocent bystanders; and that the deliberate unleashing of such destruction can only be justified by the need to defend an interest of proportionate magnitude. There will be a heavy burden of responsibility on the decisionmaker to satisfy himself that no less awful alternative would have sufficed and that the nuclear action, though horrific, was not out of proportion to the requirements of the situation.

There is room to doubt how far these internal constraints would operate on certain aspirant nuclear owners. Saddam Hussein would arguably be no more concerned with the judgment of his fellow countrymen on these than on any other matter. The Iranian theocracy (whose very different valuation of individual human life is well illustrated by the *fatwah* against Salman Rushdie) might well take a different view of the awfulness of unleashing nuclear power. But at least as far as the three recognized Western, democratic nuclear powers are concerned, the internal constraints are manifest (not only to themselves but to the world at large) and serve severely but unavoidably to limit the credibility of their deterrents in "peripheral" contexts--that is, in all cases where their fundamental national interests are not unambiguously involved. As we shall argue, this problem of credibility will be particularly acute in any attempt to deter by threatening first nuclear use in such contexts. Nuclear credibility for Western possessors depends upon a perceived proportionality between interest at stake and damage threatened; and each side of that ratio deserves closer scrutiny.

Interests: Vitality and Asymmetry

A quick mental tour of the 1990s' globe suggests remarkably few interests, away from defense of one's homeland and that of close allies and partners, that a Western nuclear power would be disposed to classify as "vital." Continued access to cheap oil supplies might be one. Defense of "kith and kin" might be another--there would, for example, probably be very few limits to the lengths to which Britain was prepared to go to assist Australia or New Zealand in the (currently unimaginable) circumstance that either found itself in mortal danger--despite the absence of any formal defense commitments. (Ties of ethnicity and culture have similarly underpinned the U.S. guarantee to Europe.)

Of course, what are intially or intrinsically peripheral interests may become more central by a process of "raising the stakes." This may be deliberate, by the undertaking of formal prior commitment to defend a region or ally (an act that puts national credibility and prestige on the table beside the original stake), or by the invocation of principle.[11] Escalation (or perhaps "quagmire") may constitute a route by which stakes are involuntarily raised--a relatively limited involvement may be transfomed by the very process of committing lives, treasure, and prestige to its pursuit into something of infinitely greater significance than the original issue. Yet, the examples of Vietnam and Afghanistan, where in each case a nuclear superpower ultimately reconciled itself to accepting defeat, suggest that the stakes in conflict are unlikely to rise sufficiently by this route to

---

[11]To choose two relatively recent examples, what the cynic might have termed an "honor" war (Britain's recapture of the Falkland Islands from Argentina) was presented as defense of the principle of self-determination, while an "oil" war in the Gulf was represented as upholding the principle of resistance to external aggression. This obviously solidifies domestic support for the conflict and impresses on the adversary the degree of one's commitment to its prosecution. But it may be doubted whether the stakes could ever be raised by these means to the point where the threat of nuclear action in their defense could seem credible. Not by accident is it "vital interests" to which people refer in discussion of nuclear deterrence, not "vital principle."

generate a perception of vital interest that nuclear weapons might legitimately defend.

These considerations underline the unlikelihood, in all but a handful of possible contingencies away from the Euro-Atlantic area, of a Western nuclear power finding itself involved in a confrontation where vital-rather-than-peripheral interests were at stake. The limitations this implies for the credibility and efficacy of any nuclear threat, implied or explicit, by such a power are reinforced by the probability that the adversary's stake in the conflict will be much larger. The examples of the Falklands and the Gulf War illustrate that, for the adversary, the conflict will in all likelihood be much closer to home, and (even if the Western power(s) publicly disavow any such purpose) will be much more likely to threaten his political if not physical survival.

Where such asymmetry of interest in a conflict exists, it must be expected that each party will be aware of it and will adjust his own behavior and expectations of the other accordingly[12]--to the detriment of Western deterrent influence. Assuming that the adversary does not himself introduce nuclear weapons into the conflict, he will calculate that the extraregional power does not have enough at stake to dispose him in reality to resort to nuclear use; that that power, moreover, will appreciate that the adversary's own interest in the conflict is such that he cannot let himself be deterred by any (almost certainly hollow) nuclear threat; and that, realizing this, the extraregional power will refrain from any attempt to bring nuclear deterrence into play in the confrontation, to avoid being forced into an unpalatable choice between having its bluff called and being manoeuvred into using nuclear weapons against its better judgment.[13]

---

[12]The classic analysis of this process of mutual accommodation of expectations and behavior is in Thomas C. Schelling, *The Strategy of Conflict,* Cambridge, Mass.: Harvard University Press, 1960.

[13]Again, the history of recent conflicts vindicates this calculation; both the Argentinean junta and Saddam Hussein clearly assumed that nuclear retaliation for their aggressions could safely be discounted, and they were right to do so. Indeed, even while the British task force sailed south to the recapture of the Falklands, the government in London made it plain that it did not see nuclear weapons

Thus the absence of a palpably vital interest, and the perception that the confrontation's outcome ultimately matters more to the adversary, will tend to negate any deterrent effect that Western nuclear powers might hope their arsenals to command in confrontation with new adversaries. But what if those adversaries are themselves nuclear-armed? Here, as noted above, the West may experience a sort of role reversal and find itself the object of an effective deterrence that forces great caution upon it in the manner in which it pursues the conflict and the extent to which it is prepared to "corner" the adversary--and perhaps even dissuades it from involvement in the first place. Consciousness of possessing a much larger nuclear arsenal may be inadequate comfort in the face of an adversary who may be prepared to "go nuclear" first, either in desperation or even, as in traditional NATO doctrine, to shock and induce a "change of heart."[14]

That said, the hypothesis of nuclear use by an adversary against a Western nuclear power--its deployed forces, its homeland (whether reached by missile or the terrorist's ingenuity) or even the forces or homeland of a nonnuclear ally--seems to suggest one type of case in which the power in question would have acquired an interest in the conflict (very likely transcending the original *casus belli*) sufficiently compelling to justify its own nuclear use. If the adversary has been the first to employ nuclear weapons, it is not hard to envisage a Western democratic leader being prepared to retaliate in kind and defend his decision subsequently--arguing the need to finish the conflict quickly, to punish the perpetrator, and to show posterity that nuclear aggression was the road to ruin.

Nor need we restrict this case solely to the hypothesis of nuclear aggression. It is at least imaginable that a use of biological or even chemical weapons that resulted in a large number of deaths, whether among combatants or civilian populations, could be seen even by Western leaders as justifying quick and overwhelming retaliation. Retaliation

---

having any bearing on the imminent conflict--just as nine years later, on the eve of the Desert Storm offensive, both the British prime minister·and the French president ruled out nuclear use.

[14]Albeit at the likely cost of suffering nuclear retaliation before the conflict was suspended.

by nuclear means in such circumstances might violate the Negative
Security Assurances (NSAs) given by all five recognized nuclear powers,
in roughly similar form, in 1978.[15] But it would seem unwise to bank on
such a pledge if, for example, the use of biological weapons had
occasioned 100,000 deaths from plague in New York, or Paris, or London.
The main function of these NSAs, perversely, may therefore be to inhibit
the nuclear-weapon states from building a form of "general" deterrence
against chemical or biological use, by making plain in advance that such
use might be met with nuclear retaliation. Nonetheless, it is at least
possible that "specific" or "immediate" nuclear deterrence could work
effectively in such circumstances--and Saddam Hussein's nonresort to
chemical weapons in the Gulf War may have been a case in point.[16]

Situations in which threats of Western nuclear first use in
response to CBW (chemical and biological weapons) attack could seem
plausible are not that hard to imagine. There are others, more
difficult to envisage and yet not perhaps to be wholly excluded. We may
find it hard in today's world to visualize the scenario in which a
sizeable Western "expeditionary force" is surrounded and threatened with
annihilation; yet, were such a situation to arise, Western leaders might
well see a "vital interest" at stake that would justify resort to

---

[15]The pledge in essence is not to use nuclear weapons against a
nonnuclear-weapon state (unless such a state is acting in alliance with
a nuclear power).

[16]Writing after the Gulf War, McGeorge Bundy ("Nuclear Weapons and
the Gulf," *Foreign Affairs*, Fall 1991) suggests that Saddam Hussein's
nonresort to chemical weapons was attributable to veiled threats of
nuclear retaliation made by the Bush administration on the eve of the
conflict. It cannot, of course, be demonstrated that the decisive
factor was fear of U.S. nuclear power, as opposed to Israeli nuclear
power, or some other cause. (Other accounts--see Lawrence Freedman and
Efraim Karsh, *The Gulf Conflict 1990-1991: Diplomacy and War in the New
World Order*, Princeton, New Jersey: Princeton University Press, 1993-
suggest that U.S. threats to widen its war objectives may have been
decisive; while Stephen Hosmer, writing in *Project AIR FORCE Annual
Report*, Santa Monica, Calif.: RAND, AR-3900-AF, 1993, attributes
Saddam's restraint to a wider policy of limiting the risks of his
confrontation with the Coalition.) But it certainly seems possible that
even if Western nuclear power fails to deter such acts of aggression as
the invasion of Kuwait, it may still be effective in constraining the
means by which the aggression is pursued.

nuclear weapons.[17] Equally, we may find it hard to imagine that some
future conflict outside Europe might be not a "theater contingency" but
the front line of a struggle against an emergent revolutionary
superpower undertaking global aggression. But after two examples of
such behavior in the twentieth century, it would seem unreasonable to
exclude totally the possibility of a third, at some indeterminate future
time.

Nuclear Damage

But, as argued above, the hypothesis of important future threats to
vital Western interests is not enough--a role for nuclear deterrence
requires also that the damage inflicted by a nuclear response could be
viewed as not utterly disproportionate. This is not a new dilemma; but
those who would advocate a role for nuclear deterrence beyond the East-
West confrontation have to face the awkward truth that what could be
contingently envisaged, in terms of levels of destruction inflicted, in
the Cold War context might now very well seem morally and politically
intolerable in relation to a threat of lesser proportions or intensity.
Allied leaders could authorize, and their publics accept or even
applaud, the dropping of atomic bombs on Japan, or the firebombing of
Dresden, because these acts occurred at the end of a prolonged life-or-
death struggle conducted on a global scale against totalitarian
societies--societies imbued with and driven by repugnant ideologies and
so comprehensively mobilized that the traditional combatant/noncombatant
distinctions of Just War theory had lost much of their force. Similar
perceptions made possible the maintenance by Western democracies,
throughout the Cold War, of nuclear target plans which, if implemented,
must intentionally or not have caused civilian deaths on a wide, perhaps
massive, scale--and without those involved in the process feeling
themselves morally deficient for doing so, given the circumstances and
the alternatives.

-----

[17]It is not necessary to debate how large the force would have to
be, only to acknowledge that there is some size of force--half a million
men, for example--for which this proposition would be true.

It seems likely, however, that the calibration of moral and
political tolerability will be considerably more difficult for those
contemplating the deterrence of the emergent "rogue" states of the
twenty-first century. Western public opinion has become more
sophisticated in its ability to draw distinctions between guilty leaders
and reluctant, perhaps terrorized, populations.[18] It is, of course,
highly uncertain how long this readiness to discriminate would survive
the onset of a truly threatening new crisis, perhaps marked by
widespread deaths, even atrocities, inflicted on Western forces or
populations. But, contemplating the "unthinkable" in the absence of
such a charged atmosphere, the Western nuclear-weapon states will have
difficulty persuading themselves that they should dispose of a credible,
i.e., contingently usable, deterrent unless they can identify ways to
target their weapons which, though threatening the destruction of assets
that the aggressor can be expected to hold very dear, would nonetheless
minimize civilian casualties and "collateral" damage.

In practice, satisfying this dual criterion may be made easier by
the fact that what the future "nuclear despot" holds most dear will very
likely *not* be his civilian population. Intolerable loss in his eyes
will more probably be those things upon which his power rests, beginning
with his own life, and perhaps embracing also his family, his tribe or
clan, along with the whole apparatus of state control--the secret
police, the ruling "party," the praetorian guard, the command-and-
control infrastructure, and possibly the military more broadly. These
are arguably the sorts of assets that would be the objects of the most
effective deterrent threats.

Yet, if we neither ought nor wish to threaten the putative
adversary's populations, then might not the type of target discussed
above be "held at risk" equally effectively, and much more credibly, by
conventional means?[19] Up to a point, perhaps--but the suggestion does

---

[18]Or even reluctant conscripts, as reflected in the Coalition's
decision to cease the destruction of the Iraqi army retreating from
Kuwait in the last days of the Gulf War.

[19]A significant literature on "conventional deterrence" has now
grown up. Seth Cropsey, "The Only Credible Deterrent," *Foreign Affairs*,
March/April 1994, has already been cited. Other recent pieces on the

not seem to do justice to the experience of the Gulf War, which demonstrated both the extent and the limitations of what can be achieved with overwhelming conventional superiority. Saddam Hussein was roundly defeated; but not even the major strategic bombing campaign effectively weakened his grip on power. The destructive potential of nuclear weapons remains greater by an order of magnitude than that of the most powerful conventional weaponry--something that gives the nuclear threat, if credited, unparalleled psychological force. Relying on the strength of his own arms, or on cunning, or on his capacity to endure the afflictions of others, the determined despot might well persuade himself that he could block, evade, absorb, or otherwise circumvent conventional assault. But there is an aura of ineluctability about the nuclear threat that is likely to make its impact on even the most headstrong aggressor, unless he is convinced that it will not be implemented.

This, however, only returns us to the dilemma of the unacceptable levels of collateral damage likely to arise from even the most limited nuclear use. For decades, weapons designers and strategists have sought escape from this dilemma by making nuclear weapons more "useable"-- smaller, more accurate, more discriminate in their effects. So the emergence at the end of the Cold War of the "mini-nuke" concept--for a new generation of very low-yield weapons that could be delivered with "surgical" accuracy by the latest precision-guidance technology--comes as no surprise. Nor is it a surprise that it should be politically stillborn. The implied requirement for new nuclear testing ran counter to the growing support for a CTB (and prompted skepticism about the motives of some of the concept's proponents). Nor would a new weapons development program sit well with the renewed international emphasis on

---

same theme include Lewis A. Dunn, "Rethinking the Nuclear Equation: The United States and the New Nuclear Powers," *The Washington Quarterly*, Winter 1994, and Charles T. Allen, "Extended Conventional Deterrence: In from the Cold and Out of the Nuclear Fire?" *The Washington Quarterly*, Summer 1994. Even now-Defense Secretary Perry, in "Desert Storm and Deterrence," *Foreign Affairs*, Fall 1991, seemed inclined to this view when he wrote, "The United States can now be confident that the defeat of a conventional armored assault in those regions [Europe and Korea] could be achieved by conventional military forces, which could enable the United States to limit the role of its nuclear forces to the deterrence of nuclear attack."

nonproliferation. Interestingly, the idea has further been condemned as not merely inopportune but also wrong *in principle*. The issues involved are explored in more detail in Appendix B. Here, we need only note that, for better or worse, no such *deus ex machina* is going to resolve the dilemma--of proportionality in the threat and use of force--that we are considering here.

If, therefore, nuclear deterrence is to have relevance in confronting new threats to international security, the Western nuclear possessors will have to persuade themselves and potential "deterrees," that they could *in extremis* pose a credibly circumscribed nuclear threat with the weapons currently available to them. No absolute answer can be given as to whether this will be possible or not. We may believe that it would be relatively easier in the case of retaliation to nuclear attack, and much harder--perhaps impossibly hard--in relation to most or all nonnuclear threats. But the precise circumstances unique to the crisis in question will be the determinant, with deterrent credibility dependent on a range of very specific technical factors--weapon effects, the type and precise location of suitable targets, population distribution, and so forth--and on the vital question with which this consideration began, of proportionality with the interest at stake. The moral and political tolerability of any use of the West's nuclear weapons, and hence the credibility of any precursive threat, will turn on circumstances--how great the menace, or the damage already sustained, or the moral outrage felt--which, away from the more predictable scenarios of Cold War confrontation, are largely unknowable in advance. It seems reasonable, if unexciting, to conclude that there will continue to be situations in the post-Cold War world in which nuclear deterrence can effectively be brought to bear--but that it will no longer be possible to identify such situations in advance with the reliability that made nuclear weapons such a force for international stability over recent decades.

THE CONTINUING RELEVANCE OF AN INDEPENDENT U.K. DETERRENT

Even, however, if a role for Western nuclear deterrence in confronting new or emergent threats is conceded--less clear-cut and less prominent than in the traditional Cold War context, but still of underlying value--the continuing need for a discrete U.K. component to that deterrence cannot be automatically assumed. Indeed, two arguments can be advanced to suggest that the independent U.K. nuclear capability is superfluous outside the European security context. First, there is the argument of the simple unlikelihood of the U.K.'s ever finding itself so seriously at odds with an extra-European power that nuclear deterrence could even enter the equation. The former Soviet threat was proximate and palpable. But why need the United Kingdom concern itself with, for example, unacceptable international behavior by a Korean or Iranian government? Britain's international responsibilities and commitments are diminishing by the year, as the long process of dismantlement of empire enters its closing stages; and the Falklands conflict demonstrated that, even where a *casus belli* may remain, neither party is likely to feel U.K. national interests to be engaged to the point where talk of nuclear weapons was remotely plausible.

This argument, however, does not look compelling. Long-term defense provision is never wisely made solely on the basis of specific, discernible threats--and no element of defense provision is more long-term than that connected with nuclear programs, where fifteen years can be required between the perception of need for a particular system and its operational availability. The difficulties of reconstructing a nuclear capability, once foresworn, under shadow of an emerging threat would be enormous, both technically and politically--to the point where nuclear renunciation, if it took place, would need to be regarded as, for all intents and purposes, for perpetuity. Yet, perpetuity is a long period over which to be confident of the absence of deadly threat, on a regional scale or even globally. Nor is it obviously safe to assume that the United Kingdom will be able to insulate itself for the indefinite future from regional dangers; though specific British commitments away from Europe may be declining, global economic interdependence and the communications revolution will make it increasingly hard for any Western country to limit its international horizons--or to decline to make appropriate contribution to the defense of the collective interests and principles of the Western democracies, when powerful challenges to them arise. Thus arguments based on "purely" U.K. interests, and the likelihood or otherwise of menace to them, fail to recognize the extent to which those interests may be bound up with wider collective interests, which it is much less easy to assume will be indefinitely immune to aggression. And, as noted above, in a world of proliferation, there can be no guarantees that the stakes which justify the initial commitment of force will not be dramatically raised by the development of the conflict itself.

This argument suggests that future U.K. involvement in deadly armed confrontation should not be discounted. But it also suggests that the most probable context would be a Coalition action such as that undertaken against Saddam Hussein. In that case, the United States could be expected to be fully engaged (U.S. leadership seeming to be a likely indispensable condition for any such action), and U.S. nuclear power could be expected to be available to influence the conflict to the extent that Western nuclear deterrence comes into play at all. In the classic Cold War situation, the reliability of U.S. extended deterrence could conceivably be questioned, given the vulnerability of the U.S. homeland. But such uncertainties would have no place in a confrontation with a "third world" proliferator, lacking intercontinental ballistic missiles (ICBMs) with which to pose a threat to the United States. The old "second center of nuclear decisionmaking" thesis does not translate out of the Cold War context--nor, therefore, does the requirement for an independent U.K. deterrent.

Of course, the currently relatively small number of countries with ICBM capabilities is a tenuous basis upon which to build a thesis of U.S. invulnerability. Nor, of course, are such missiles the only methods of "delivering" nuclear or other relevant weapons. A nuclear warhead might equally be conveyed to the United States by a freighter-- or a biological agent, by the diplomatic pouch. It would seem wrong, therefore, to imagine that the United States could in future confront some aggressive regional power, certainly one among the growing band disposing of nuclear, biological, or chemical (NBC) weapons without acute concerns not only for U.S. forces deployed in theater but also for the U.S. homeland itself.

However, the same arguments of vulnerability apply with equal force to the United Kingdom. Moreover, in future coalition actions against aggressive regional powers, there would be no basis for assuming that U.K. interests would be more threatened than those of the United States--as arguably might have been the case with a Soviet invasion of Europe. These considerations, rather than any picture of U.S. invulnerability, render implausible an argument on the lines of "a future Saddam might discount U.S. nuclear action, but he could not be so certain about the British."

All this said, to conclude that in such nontraditional contexts there would be no U.S. "credibility gap" that Britain would be well placed to plug is not necessarily to conclude that there would be no "value added" in a U.K. deterrent. First, the "second center" thesis might still continue to apply, in the attenuated form that confrontation with two rather that one Western nuclear possessor would simply give the adversary more to think about. Second, and more compelling, is the argument of solidarity. It seems clear that, at the conventional level, the United States would greatly welcome, and be much more disposed to take action if it obtained, assistance and a sharing of responsibility by key Allies. If this proves true, then in a crisis sufficiently dire to acquire a nuclear dimension, the solidarity of Allies with matching capabilities and parallel responsibilities would be invaluable. As with support at the conventional level, the significance of such burden sharing might be as much moral and political as practical; but it would be none the less effective for that. The importance of such moral solidarity is well brought out by Robert Levine's image[20] of the United States acting in the post-Cold War world (he has of course the context of Uniform Deterrence of nuclear use specifically in mind) less as a global policeman than as a global sheriff--accepting a duty to take the initiative in dealing with outlaws, but only to the extent that others make themselves available to serve on the posse. The United States could not reasonably be expected to bear alone the full moral and political burden of underpinning the defense of Western values and

---

[20]Op. cit.

interests in the face of nuclear or other mortal threats in all
circumstances and indefinitely.

CONCLUSION

This section has argued that there is no *a priori* reason why
nuclear deterrence should not operate in situations other than the
familiar East-West context, the context in which deterrent notions and
doctrines were originally framed. For example, there is no reason to
doubt that those states with whom the Western democracies might at some
future point find themselves in conflict understand basic deterrent
logic. However, absent a developed mutual understanding of the limits
of tolerable behavior, the application of nuclear deterrence will
involve greater risks. The asymmetry of interest that may mark
confrontations between "rogue" states and a Western coalition may make
it harder to conceive of a nuclear use that would be justifiable, or to
frame a nuclear threat that would be credible; and even if the threat is
credible, that same asymmetry of interest may make the threat inadequate
for successful deterrence.

The comparative rarity of reasonably foreseeable cases in which
truly vital Western interests were at stake, and the difficulty of
threatening nuclear damage that would not be self-evidently morally and
politically intolerable, suggest that deterrence may be more effective
in such circumstances at constraining the manner in which conflicts are
conducted (that is, in deterring nuclear and perhaps other WMD use by
the adversary) than at preventing their occurrence in the first place.
We need not feel that nuclear weapons have no deterrent capability
outside Cold War Europe; but neither can we plausibly maintain the claim
for them, outside that context, that they "prevent *any* kind of war." In
such circumstances, a policy of deterrence clearly cannot bear the
whole--perhaps not even the main--weight of counterproliferation
strategy; for those purposes, recourse must be had to the full spectrum
of policies of denial, dissuasion, and defense available to make the
acquisition of weapons of mass destruction more difficult and less
appealing. Within these constrained conditions the independent U.K.
nuclear deterrent can be ascribed a modest potential utility, most

probably in moral and political support of U.S. deterrent power. But this modest role would scarcely seem to equate to a potential "new rationale" for the U.K. deterrent, even if it were not politically inopportune to assert it. This conclusion, if accepted, seems to direct us back once more to the European context in search of a satisfactory rationale.

6. A "EURODETERRENT"?

The ending of the Cold War has weakened the old rationale for British nuclear weapons as a contribution to NATO collective deterrence. We have therefore looked beyond NATO's horizons to see whether the purpose of the British deterrent might be redefined in relation to a wider international environment. We have considered whether Britain's nuclear capability might not be rededicated to the enhancement of global security--either by showing the way to marginalize nuclear force in international affairs, or, conversely, by acting as a deterrent to new forms and sources of aggression. The failure to find a wholly satisfying answer in either direction suggests that the rationale that carries the U.K. deterrent forward into the twenty-first century may need to be essentially Eurocentric.

As we saw in the preceding section, this is certainly the line to which the current Conservative government seems determined to stick. Its persuasiveness depends upon how the security situation of Europe is perceived--and it has been significantly diminished by the collapse of the threat from the East. But, it may be argued, this is not the only current development in European security of fundamental importance. Potentially just as significant, albeit over a longer time frame, is the emergence of a more closely integrated Europe, ready to take on progressively greater responsibility for its own defense within a rebalanced Atlantic Alliance. The launching of the European Union commits the 12 member states to the development of a European Security and Defense Identity (ESDI), tending ultimately toward a common defense. Yet, can this vision of an eventual common defense be conceived without the underpinning of a European nuclear capability? As the February 1994 French White Paper on Defense expresses it, "With nuclear potential, Europe's autonomy with regard to defense is possible; without it, it is not." Might it not therefore be in this context that the U.K. nuclear deterrent will increasingly be seen to have its principal value?

DEVELOPMENTS TO DATE

Of the two European nuclear-weapon states, France has been much the more forward-thinking in this area. As David Yost has noted, various ideas were floated in the 1980s for a West European nuclear planning group for consultations about the British and French forces, without ever getting onto the political agenda.[1] The end of the Cold War and the unification of Germany transformed the situation. Ever ready to doubt the U.S. commitment to Europe, French security thinkers began to worry about the future nuclear protection of the united Germany. In July 1990, Defense Minister Chevènement suggested that a West European defense partnership offering nuclear protection to Germany was the only choice, given the alternatives: "An American protection that risks seeming more and more uncertain? Or Germany's choice to secure her security by herself?"[2]

The new international situation had, however, brought France even more fundamental nuclear preoccupations than concern for Germany's security choices. Like Britain, France confronted a crisis of nuclear identity; unlike Britain, she could not seek refuge in the declared commitment of her nuclear weapons to the service of a wider Alliance that had, "reduced reliance" notwithstanding, reaffirmed its continuing importance. For France, her nuclear capability had always been a symbol of national sovereignty and independence--in an international climate disposed to ask new questions about the purpose and legitimacy of nuclear possession, this was an uncomfortably exposed position.

The upshot has been a far-reaching series of changes to French nuclear plans and policies. In July 1991, President Mitterrand cancelled plans to replace the aging *Plateau d'Albion* silo-based missiles with the S45, a mobile land-based version of the M45 missile to be deployed in the new *Triomphant* class of nuclear missile submarines. In June 1992, the planned production of those boats was itself reduced from six to four (the first is due in service in 1995), and it was

---

[1]David S. Yost, *Western Europe and Nuclear Weapons,* Livermore, California: Center for Security and Technology Studies, Lawrence Livermore National Laboratory, University of California, 1993.

[2]Interview, *Le Monde*, July 13, 1990.

announced that the minimum number of missile submarines to be maintained on patrol at any one time would drop from three to two. Acquisition of nuclear-capable fighter-bombers was cut back; and, most striking of all, the short-range Hades ground-to-ground missile project was terminated when only 30 of the intended 120 missiles had been produced.[3] In parallel, and for the first time, the budget for the French nuclear program has declined in real terms--not least because of the Gulf War's exposure of significant deficiencies in France's conventional and intelligence capabilities as a consequence of the nuclear element's preemption of the lion's share of defense funding over the years (as discussed in Section 3 above).

Even more striking have been the policy shifts, starting with the June 1991 announcement that France would accede to the NPT. The following April came the French declaration of a moratorium on nuclear testing--a move which contributed materially to the erosion of support for testing in the U.S. Congress and the October 1992 U.S. legislation for the conclusion of the Comprehensive Test Ban Treaty and a final end to all testing. For the British (who had made no secret of their lack of enthusiasm for this tide of events), the fact of having this French presidential initiative sprung upon them with no prior warning was made only marginally less painful by the realization that the entire French government, excepting only Prime Minister Bérégovoy, had been similarly blind-sided.

It is certainly ironic that, of the three Western nuclear powers, France is probably least well placed to cope without further nuclear tests; she has at least three new warheads, or warhead appplications, in prospect,[4] and is probably less advanced than either the United States or the United Kingdom in the development of alternatives to testing, whether simulation or computer modelling.[5] Nonetheless, having

---

[3]David Yost has traced the interesting confusion surrounding this cancellation--op. cit., p. 8. Contrary to initial impressions, it seems that the 30 missiles produced have been mothballed, not scrapped.

[4]For the M45 missile, for the follow-on M5 missile planned for 2010, and for a possible air-to-ground nuclear standoff missile.

[5]France's PALEN program (Préparation à la Limitation des Expérimentations Nucléaires) was established only in 1991. See the speech on *Deterrence* delivered at the Elysée palace on May 5, 1994, by

initiated the chain reaction, the Elysée subsequently (July 4, 1993) had little choice but to bite the bullet and declare support for a Comprehensive Test Ban Treaty, provided that it was "universal and verifiable."

These shifts and changes, from a country that previously prided itself on walking alone in nuclear matters, constitute a changed behavioral pattern that might almost be construed as a loss of nerve. French commentators dwell anxiously on the issue of the "legitimacy" of France's nuclear deterrence.[6] Such misgivings no doubt contributed to France's uncharacteristic readiness to associate herself with most of NATO's new Strategic Concept (see Section 2) and to soft-pedal the traditional differentiation of French nuclear policy from that of her allies. But it is in the idea of European defense that French opinion has evidently seen the most promising cause to which the French deterrent might be rededicated.

As noted above, this is not a new idea; but it received major new impetus when, in January 1992, Mitterrand mused publicly on the future of the European Community in the following terms: "Only two of the twelve have an atomic force. For their national policy, they have a clear doctrine. Is it possible to conceive a European doctrine? This question will very rapidly become one of the major questions in the construction of a joint European defense."[7] No consultation with the United Kingdom preceded this trial balloon, and none followed it; but the theme was taken up in the French press, and achieved sufficient currency to create an expectation that, when Defence Secretary Rifkind agreed to speak at his French counterpart's syposium on the new strategic environment in September that year in Paris, he would provide a British "response" to these French "proposals."

President Mitterrand--a good summary of the state of France's various nuclear programs.

[6]See, for example, the sources quoted by David S. Yost, "Nuclear Weapons Issues in France," in John C. Hopkins and Weixing Hu, eds., *Strategic Views from the Second Tier: The Nuclear Weapons Policies of France, Britain, and China*, San Diego: Institute on Global Conflict and Cooperation, University of California, 1994.

[7]François Mitterrand, speech at the Palais des Congrès, Paris, January 10, 1992.

In truth, the British reaction was very mixed. Though the U.K. rationale for nuclear ownership remained firmly NATO-centric, one outcome could be significant attraction in reinforcing the case by representing the two European deterrent forces as being also at the service of the wider European community (or Community). Cooperation with France on this basis would lend substance to the United Kingdom's protestations of determination to occupy a place "at the very heart of Europe"[8]--at a time when so much of British European policy looked more insular than *communautaire*. Another outcome could be the added satisfaction of moving closer to France in a field where Germany could play no leading role; nuclear cooperation across the Channel could be a valuable counterpoise to wider Franco-German partnership within the Community. With defense budgets under increasing pressure, there was every incentive to see whether closer collaboration between Europe's two nuclear powers could yield mutual technical and financial advantage. Finally, though the British might be less ready than the French to anticipate U.S. disengagement from Europe, the possibility of a diminishing U.S. commitment to the defense of Europe and/or to the U.S.-U.K. nuclear defense relationship could not be wholly excluded; the development of closer cross-Channel links was arguably a sensible hedging strategy. It was a strategy, too, with a certain psychological attraction--the pleasure of a new flirtation.

On the other hand, there was also an acute awareness of the risks that flirtation with Paris could hold for a relationship with Washington on nuclear issues that was of such long-standing and intimacy as to be almost matrimonial. Indeed, the nuclear question was itself a subset of the wider dilemma of how sense and substance could be imparted to the ESDI without damaging the transatlantic cohesion of NATO. The Maastricht Treaty on European Union betrayed the divergence of Member States' views, with its tortured pronouncement that, "The common foreign and security policy shall include all questions related to the security

---

[8]Speech by Prime Minister Major in Bonn, March 11, 1991--his first speech outside the United Kingdom after succeeding the "Eurosceptical" Margaret Thatcher and intended to signal a more cooperative British approach to Europe.

of the Union, including the eventual framing of a common defence policy, which might in time lead to a common defence." At this overarching level, the British position was, and remains, clear: the ESDI, whatever it comes to amount to, should be developed not as something antithetical to NATO but as a strengthened European "pillar" *within* an Atlantic Alliance rebalanced by a more prominent European contribution to the common defense. Consistent with that approach, the United Kingdom worked hard to ensure that the new EuroCorps, with its "European vocation," should continue to be available to NATO; and the imperative of maintaining Alliance solidarity was felt to apply with even greater force in the nuclear domain.

These, then, were the sort of contradictory considerations and impulses which bore on the British reaction to France's oblique overtures. The initial synthesis was set out in Malcolm Rifkind's speech to the Joxe symposium in September 1992. He was explicit in his disavowal of interest in any form of "Eurodeterrence" defined by the exclusion of the United States, or in "exploring hypotheses about what might happen in the absence of a U.S. commitment--both nuclear and conventional--to the defense of Europe. The Atlantic Alliance exists, and will continue to exist, at the centre of our strategic thinking."[9] Nonetheless, Rifkind went on to express his vision of "the opportunity and challenge for Europe being to contribute more fully to supporting the collective deterrence;" and he outlined two ways in which this might be done.

The first was "a steadily closer cooperation and cohesion between the two Western European nuclear powers." This, he felt, was not just a matter of likely mutual benefit, but something that could represent a powerful underpinning to collective deterrence within the Alliance as

---

[9]To ensure that his message was clearly understood, he continued: "for Europe and America to develop separate security strategies would be in the interests of neither continent. It is not in our security interests to encourage any tendency towards thinking that there could be a major conflict in Europe in which the question of nuclear use arose which did not involve the vital interests of all the allies including the United States."

well, "by demonstrating identity of interest and purpose between NATO's European nuclear powers."

A second route to a strengthening of the European contribution to deterrence might lie, Rifkind suggested, in "a clearer perception that the weapons of the European nuclear powers are there not merely to protect the national interests of Britain and France narrowly defined, but to underpin the security of nonnuclear partners and allies as well." Collective deterrence could only be the stronger the more it was apparent that Britain and France each regarded her vital interests as inextricably entwined with those of her European partners and allies.[10] He reminded his French audience that Britain already achieved this by its commitment of its nuclear capability to SACEUR, for the common Alliance defense; and, though he explicitly denied any intention to invite France to follow suit, he implied that, if France was keen to promote "Eurodeterrence," an important prerequisite would be for France to cease to talk of her nuclear capability as exclusively the expression and instrument of French national sovereignty and to make plain that she saw those vital interests to which her nuclear power was relevant as effectively encompassing the whole of Western Europe.

In effect, therefore, Rifkind parried the implication of the French initiative, that it was for the British to join them in a European enterprise, by suggesting that in the area of guaranteeing the security of European partners France had some catching up to do. Nonetheless, his speech was accepted as a serious attempt to engage on the issue and was welcomed in Paris as such--as was the simultaneous announcement that the two countries had agreed to make a concerted new effort to align more closely their nuclear policies and doctrines. To this end, the Franco-British Joint Commission on Nuclear Policy and Doctrine was established, bringing together senior officials from respective foreign and defense ministries.

Not a great deal has been said publicly about the progress of this effort. However, following the Franco-British Summit on July 26, 1993,

---

[10]There was a degree of no doubt deliberate ambiguity about whether Rifkind had here primarily in mind the other members of the European Community--"partners," or NATO's European members--"allies."

John Major described the objective as being "to coordinate our approach
to deterrence, to nuclear doctrine and concepts, antimissile defenses,
arms control and nonproliferation," and noted that "we have decided
today to make this Joint Commission a permanent standing body, with a
substantial amount of work to continue into the future." The
institutionalization of the body makes plain that the first year's work
had been productive and that both countries remained keen (despite the
substitution of Gaullist for socialist government in France in the
meantime) to pursue the nuclear *entente*.[11] And British policymakers
will have been pleased more recently to note in the new French Defense
White Paper both a call for enhanced cooperation with Britain in the
context of European defense, and a specific reference to the nuclear
dialogue as something to be "pursued and deepened."[12]

SCOPE FOR FURTHER FRANCO-BRITISH COOPERATION

The evidence therefore is that the process of alignment of policy,
doctrine, and strategic view is proceeding to both governments'
satisfaction. What is less clear is whether on this occasion, any more
than in the past, it will prove possible to reinforce a closer nuclear
relationship with practical benefits flowing from technical or
operational cooperation. At the technical level it might seem self-
evident that closer cooperation between two small nuclear-weapon states
must make for reciprocal benefit, through the sharing of overheads and
economies of scale. In practice, the fact that the respective programs,
and accompanying design and production approaches have developed
independently and on different lines will act as a constraint. The

---

[11]In his King's College speech in November 1993, Malcolm Rifkind
spoke approvingly of the Commission's work which, he suggested, had
confirmed that "there are no differences between France and the United
Kingdom on the fundamental nuclear issues."

[12]p. 56. They will also have noted with approval evidence of a
conditional willingness to broaden the concept of France's "vital
national interests" in very much the way that Rifkind had urged. See
pp. 24-25: "We must not, however, lose sight of the questions opened by
the perspective of the construction of a common European defense within
the framework of European Union. It cannot indeed be ruled out, in the
long term, that to the extent that the interests of the European nations
converge, so France's concept of her vital national interests may come
to coincide with that of her neighbors."

United Kingdom will also want to be careful to observe the prohibition in the U.S.-U.K. 1958 Agreement against dissemination to third parties of information obtained under the agreement.[13]

Despite these constraints, fruitful collaboration should still be possible, given the political will--perhaps particularly in the development of alternative techniques to live testing, such as simulation and computer modeling. Each country will find it difficult to adapt to a world without tests (and in particular to underwrite the continuing safety of its nuclear stockpile in such conditions), and yet may find it easier to cooperate in this field of "alternatives" where the subject matter is at one remove from actual weapon design. There should be scope to develop collaboration in this area without cutting across the U.S.-U.K. relationship, though many would argue that, if the politics can be made to fit, the most logical arrangement would be some sort of *ménage à trois* between the Western nuclear-weapon states.

At the operational level, it is sometimes suggested that Britain and France could demonstrate greater nuclear solidarity by coordinating the patrols of their nuclear missile submarines and/or perhaps undertaking some form of joint targeting. The former idea has little, in practice, to commend it. Despite the significant cutbacks in their nuclear forces and alert levels since the end of the Cold War, both Britain and France currently regard it as axiomatic that they should retain at least one (and in France's case at least two) nuclear missile submarines at sea at all times, so that a necessary minimum national nuclear retaliatory capability is always available, invulnerable to preemption. As long as each of the two governments adheres to this national policy, there will be nothing to coordinate. Only if both agreed that the security of each could be adequately guaranteed by the presence at sea of a submarine of the other could the question of

---

[13]This factor would very probably rule out the idea (which had a brief currency at the time when it seemed that France might in due course resume nuclear testing) that if Nevada were unavailable, Britain might instead conduct further nuclear tests at France's test site in the South Pacific. The testing process involves such intimate disclosure of the design of the device under test that any such arrangement would have been very difficult without falling foul of the 1958 Agreement's stipulations.

coordination arise. Such an arrangement would, if publicized, amount to a dramatic demonstration of Franco-British mutual reliance in the nuclear area. But the practical benefits, in terms of savings from further relaxation of each nation's submarine patrolling patterns, would be small, and certainly inconsequential compared with the mountain each government would have to climb in explaining to its national legislature and public why it had decided to entrust the ultimate guaranteeing of its own national security to the head of government of the other in, so to speak, alternate months. For now, the idea looks a nonstarter.

The reference above to national minimum nuclear retaliatory capabilities suggests, however, one possible line of doctrinal evolution. The doctrine of "minimum sufficiency" in deterrence to which both countries subscribe requires that each country maintains the ability to inflict on any potential aggressor damage outweighing any gain he could hope to achieve. The British government, at any rate, has made it plain that this criterion is taken seriously in the sizing of the British nuclear deterrent force.[14] But, while it is easy to see how forces may be sized to threaten a specific level of damage, it is less clear what assumptions can or should be made about the extent of the gain that that damage is intended, potentially, to outweigh. Should Britain (or, indeed, France) aim to hold out a retaliatory threat on a scale that would make aggression against its specific national territory unattractive by comparison--or is it aggression on a larger scale, aimed at the whole of Western Europe, that the national deterrent, single-handed, is meant to be able to render unacceptably risky?

Neither British nor French government has ever been explicit on this point. No wonder, since calculations in this area must inevitably be extremely assumption-heavy and by-and-large. Nonetheless, it would seem not illogical, to put it no more strongly, if the British and French governments, each pronouncing its own minimum nuclear forces

---

[14]See the government response to a parliamentary question on the criteria for determining Trident warhead numbers: "Trident will deploy the minimum number of warheads necessary to provide effective deterrence, presenting the prospect of damage no aggressor could find acceptable." House of Commons Official Report, February 25, 1992, col. 452.

adequate for direct protection of specifically national interests,
further suggested that their combined weights should be adequate to
counterbalance in the mind of any aggressor even the gains that might
flow from aggression against Western Europe as a whole. To impart
substance to such a doctrine would require the organization of
complementary targeting by the two countries--something that need not be
incompatible with the maintenance of separate national targeting plans
or, indeed, plans coordinated with NATO. If Richard Ullman's account[15]
is to be believed, France has long covertly maintained two sets of
strategic target plans, one coordinated with SACEUR and one for
independent action. If two, why not three, the third coordinated with
the United Kingdom?

Such arrangements would certainly do much to cement the bilateral
nuclear relationship. Though both governments would probably wish to
preserve their current positions of declining to discuss detailed
targeting issues, they could make it publicly plain that they were
taking steps to ensure that their respective deterrent forces were
operationally compatible, so as to constitute a properly complementary
contribution to the collective deterrence. And they could affirm their
belief that the combined potential of their two nuclear forces should be
adequate to deter major aggression not merely against their own vital
national interests but against those of their European partners and
allies as well. Nor need such a doctrine be taken to imply the
exclusion or superfluity of U.S. deterrent power--redundancy of mutual
support between members of a defensive alliance is, after all, an asset
to be valued.

Such a doctrine might in due course commend itself to London and
Paris, if and as the nuclear *entente* develops--but not now. In the
absence of any clearly discernible threat of major aggression to Western
Europe, its articulation would seem irrelevant; and the process of
European integration still has a considerable distance to travel before
the idea of a Franco-British nuclear guarantee could begin to acquire
plausibility. For the moment, the two governments can be expected to

---

[15]Richard H. Ullman, "The French Connection," *Foreign Policy*,
Summer 1989.

pursue their dialogue in a low-key fashion and with no large claims. Among the factors determining whether it develops over time a more self-consciously European character will be the attitudes of friends and allies.

ATTITUDES OF FRIENDS AND ALLIES

As noted above, from the U.K. perspective the most important of allies will be the United States. Nuclear dependencies apart, it would go against long-established U.K. instincts to undertake a major departure or initiative in international security policy of which the United States positively disapproved. Recent developments have, however, been reassuring on this score. The January 1994 NATO Summit marked an important step forward toward reconciling the future roles of NATO and the ESDI, much along the lines that the British had been advocating. The Summit Declaration recorded "full support to the development of a European Security and Defence Identity which . . . might in time lead to a common defence compatible with that of the Atlantic Alliance. The emergence of a European Security and Defence Identity will strengthen the European pillar of the Alliance while reinforcing the transatlantic link and will enable European allies to take greater responsibility for their common security and defence."[16]

Thus the Summit outcome demonstrated a new U.S. readiness to see the ESDI develop and a new French readiness to see that happen in a fashion complementary to NATO; and both these circumstances will have encouraged the United Kingdom to feel that it has latitude to pursue its nuclear dialogue with France without having to be overly concerned about the risk of hostile U.S. reaction. A further, perverse, kind of encouragement may derive from the poor state of overall Anglo-American relations, discussed in Section 3. In the past, London has often seemed more royalist even than the king in opposing any development in European

---

[16]At the operational level this reconciliation was reflected in the Summit's expressed support for "the development of separable but not separate capabilities which could respond to European requirements and contribute to Alliance security" (the "Eurocorps" was principally in mind here), and in the concept of Combined Joint Task Forces--a device whereby primarily European operations could, if nations so chose, make use of Alliance assets.

security that could conceivably tend to the exclusion of the United States. But if the bilateral relationship with Washington fails to recapture past warmth and intimacy, then the United Kingdom may gradually show itself less solicitous of the transatlantic link and increasingly ready to see how the ESDI can be developed. This will be especially true if bilateral coolness contributes to a perception in London that U.S. indulgence of the ESDI concept is in fact a manifestation of an underlying wish to disengage from foreign, or at least European, entanglements. In the same way, any further evidence of an American desire to orchestrate the "delegitimization" of Western nuclear possession will tend to push the British in the direction of France.

Also important will be the views of nonnuclear partners and allies. British and French nuclear deterrents can be plausibly represented as serving the defense interests of their European partners only if those partners are content to have it so. Yet, partners such as the Germans and the Italians show no current readiness to subscribe to this approach. German attitudes in particular would be crucial, and the evidence is that they have little current interest in acknowledgement of the protection of some sort of Franco-British nuclear umbrella in a European context.

As noted in Section 4, German repudiation of nuclear weapons seems more solid than ever. Far from wanting them for themselves (as Jean-Pierre Chevènement [see above] feared), postunification public opinion polls have suggested that 70 percent of Germans favor the removal of even the remaining U.S. nuclear weapons from their soil.[17] Though none of the German political parties is disposed to rock the Alliance boat on the issue, the dominant German view appears to be that, with the ending of the Cold War, nuclear weapons have become for all practical purposes an irrelevancy. Thus, whatever view Germans might take of the continuing need for U.S. extended deterrence guarantees, they can not be expected to take kindly to the United Kingdom and France attempting to award themselves leadership roles in the developing European Union on

---

[17]See Ronald D. Asmus, *Germany in Transition: National Confidence and International Reticence*, Santa Monica, Calif.: RAND, P-7767, 1992.

the strength of their nuclear capabilities. This attitude is plainly
evidenced by those German interlocutors who recently explained to David
Yost that they had no interest in some sort of extended Franco-British
nuclear guarantee since "by definition, lesser powers cannot guarantee
the security of a greater power."[18]

Selling "Eurodeterrence" to Germany would not, then, be an easy
task, even if the pitch soft-pedalled the military/strategic case and
aimed instead to persuade Germans that, politically, a collective
deterrent was an essential part of Europe's coming-of-age. Such an
approach could succeed only if the means were available to make Franco-
British nuclear forces "European" in more than merely nominal terms--
that is, to involve other European partners at least as closely as nonnuclear NATO Allies have been associated with U.S. extended deterrence
in Europe through the "burden-sharing" arrangements. Conceivably, had
France and Britain decided to collaborate on a new air-to-ground standoff nuclear missile, such a project could have become the vehicle for a
wider European cooperation. It would have been hard for their European
partners to subscribe to nuclear modernization; but arrangements for the
deployment and delivery of such a missile, perhaps even its acquisition,
might have been framed to maximize participation of nonnuclear partners
short of direct operational control. Such possibilities disappeared,
however, with the British decision in October 1993 not to proceed with
the missile project. In its absence, it is not easy to see how
practical arrangements could be framed to give nonnuclear European
partners a proper "ownership stake" in a "European" nuclear policy.

To put the matter another way and pick up an institutional proposal
sometimes advanced by advocates of Eurodeterrence, if a European
equivalent of NATO's Nuclear Planning Group were to be established, what
could there be for it to discuss? In current circumstances, the
interest of the majority might well be as much in constraining as in
sharing in the French and British deterrent capabilities. Ironically,
this suggests a rather different sort of European nuclear

---

[18]See David S. Yost, *Western Europe and Nuclear Weapons*, Livermore,
California: Center for Security and Technology Studies, Lawrence
Livermore National Laboratory, University of California, 1993, p. 18.

"responsibility-sharing" arrangement--one designed to accommodate more European fingers not on the nuclear trigger but on the safety catch. NATO's stillborn Multilateral Force would be the obvious, if inauspicious, precedent--an arrangement designed to give the nonnuclear European allies control of nuclear weapons in the sense of the power not to initiate but to prevent launch. It could not be expected that such "negative control" arrangements could be applied to the entirety of the British and French national arsenals (any more than the MLF encompassed more than a fraction of the U.S. arsenal)--and even that would be hard for the two nuclear powers to accept.[19] But it might at least provide for the Germans, Italians, and others the sort of locus to influence the planning and policies of their nuclear partners that is likely to be the minimum they will require in exchange for the ackowledgment of a specifically European role for the U.K. and French deterrents.

The very obvious difficulties in all this suggest that any nuclear dimension that the ESDI may one day come to obtain is much more likely to come at the end of a long process of integration of conventional forces and policies than to be the element of European security policy that sets the pace. It will be many years, if at all, before British governments can describe the primary purpose of the national deterrent as the underpinning of the security of the European Union. For now, the possible future European dimension is a legitimate, but in itself inadequate, element in the case for the U.K. deterrent.

---

[19]The Gaullist maxim that "le nucléaire ne se partage pas" has recently been reaffirmed by President Mitterrand, in his speech of May 5, 1994, at the Elysée Palace: "France's nuclear weapons . . . depend on French decision, and French decision alone."

7. SOME POLICY IMPLICATIONS

A "BLESSING IN DISGUISE" FOR EUROPEAN SECURITY

It is time to take stock. We have noted (against the background that the United Kingdom will in all probability remain a nuclear-weapon state for at least the next two or three decades) a need for the traditional rationale to be reinforced or replaced--not least for the sake of Britain's relations with the United States. We have therefore considered three possible ways in which the rationale might be redefined.

The "catalyst for denuclearization" concept would switch the emphasis away from the deterrent potential of Britain's nuclear weapons to their possible utility as a means to encourage nuclear disarmament and discourage nuclear proliferation. But our analysis questioned the effectiveness of such an approach. Its direct and indirect effects seemed more likely to work to the detriment of international security, by weakening NATO's ability to deter aggression and by providing a perverse incentive to proliferation. We therefore considered the alternative proposition that it is to the deterrence of "new threats," such as those from proliferation, that the U.K. nuclear capability should be rededicated. But this did not convince us, either: though our analysis did not exclude a useful role for Western deterrent power outside the traditional East-West context, or the possible value of a specifically British contribution, the uncertainties seemed too great for this to be persuasive as the main rationale for the U.K.'s nuclear weapons. Nor would such a new rationale seem politic: while the postures of the recognized nuclear-weapon states might in practice have very little bearing on the calculations of regional proliferators, there was a good argument for refraining from handing them easy justifications for their actions.

These considerations suggest that the best future rationale for the U.K. deterrent will probably, like its traditional predecessor, remain Eurocentric; and we therefore considered whether the U.K. deterrent might acquire a "European vocation," as an underpinning of the common

European defense that European Union may one day entail. We found some attraction in this proposition--but as a rather distant perspective, dependent on prior progress with wider European integration. For now, the most that it may be possible (politically and realistically) to claim in this context for the British and French deterrent capabilities is that their progressively closer coordination would represent a strengthened European contribution to the Atlantic Alliance's collective deterrence.

Such, indeed, is broadly the line that British ministers currently seem disposed to pursue. The case for continued U.K. nuclear possession is pinned to cautious preservation of a North Atlantic security framework that has served to keep the peace for nearly half a century, complemented by the suggestion of a more specifically European rationale that might emerge over time. The preceding analysis suggests that this approach may be about the best that is currently available. It seems intellectually sustainable; and it seems likely to command both French support and at least U.S. tolerance. Critically, and as an essential condition of this last conclusion, the approach avoids making any large claims about the relevance of nuclear deterrence in the wider world that could provide comfort to proliferators.

In Section 3, we drew a distinction between two fundamentally opposed attitudes to the role of nuclear weapons in international security--the one regarding them as a sort of Blessing in Disguise, the other viewing them as the Ultimate Evil. The foregoing analysis suggests that the right approach for the United Kingdom will be to continue to assert a Blessing in Disguise view of nuclear deterrence in the Euro-Atlantic context (and to sustain a suite of nuclear policies consistent with that view), while soft-pedalling any such claims in relation to extra-European security.

The wisdom of this last point can be illustrated by considering what a Blessing in Disguise posture in relation to wider-world security might amount to and what its consequences might be expected to be. As suggested earlier, the posture need not amount to any simplistic "the more the better" attitude to nuclear proliferation. It might instead express itself in terms of a sort of "brutal realism," arguing that the best hope for the maintenance of relative stability in the international order rests on the existence in a limited number of hands of the ultimate sanction of nuclear force. Arguments about discrimination and inequity would be met by the assertion that what matters is not abstract fairness but what works in practice; that the five recognized nuclear powers have given proof of their responsibility and restraint over thirty years and more; and that the distinction between nuclear-weapon and non-nuclear-weapon states, mere product of historical accident though it may be, is enshrined in the NPT--a treaty to which over 160 nations have so far judged it pragmatically in their best interests to adhere.

Developing the theme, the "brutal realist" might go on to recall that, although the NPT requires the five nuclear-weapon states to pursue nuclear disarmament (as they have conspicuously done of late), it postpones the ultimate elimination of such weapons to the unrealizable context of "general and complete disarmament." He could emphasize (picking up the arguments considered in Section 4) that the international nonproliferation regime is not some sort of favor done for the nuclear-weapon states by the non-nuclear-weapon states. On the contrary, the NNWS arguably benefit by it even more than the NWS. Historical chance has selected a limited number of trustees of nuclear power; everyone is better off if that number remains limited; and everyone would in actuality be worse off if such trustees did not exist. Nor should the trustees be envied their responsibilities; maintaining the necessary sanction of ultimate force involves them in both cost and risk.

The point of setting out this line of argument is not to assess how far it might be valid, and how far merely self-serving. Rather, it is to illustrate its political untenability. Altruistic assumption of global nuclear duties might seem an heroic posture in the short term, but could backfire catastrophically if the promissory note were ever called in. Nor, even in the short term, would there be any thanks from the international community on offer. On the contrary, such an insensitive approach would be a short road to wrecking the 1995 NPT extension conference; and, if it emanated now from a British government, would cause major difficulties with Washington. For British governments, the moral is clear: advocacy of the enduring Blessing in Disguise aspect to the British nuclear deterrent should be confined to the specifically European context. Outside that context, Britain will do well to avoid large claims for the role of nuclear-weapon states in the maintenance of international security. Rather, it should back U.S. efforts to curb regional proliferation, whether in North East Asia, in the Middle East, or in the Subcontinent. Initiatives that seem pragmatically sensible in that regard--the negotiation of further nuclear-weapon-free zones, to take one example, or efforts to cap existing arsenals--should be supported. Nothing should be claimed for nuclear weapons which could justify proliferators or undermine U.S. antiproliferation efforts.

REASONS TO REJECT AN "ULTIMATE EVIL" CONCEPT ELSEWHERE

Does this amount to advocating a "Blessing in Disguise in the European context, Ultimate Evil elsewhere" position on nuclear weapons? It does not. There are at least three reasons why it would be a mistake to rush to the other side of the intellectual boat, and deprecate Western nuclear capabilities in all international contexts except that of European security.

The 1995 NPT Extension Conference

The first reason relates to the NPT extension conference. Here there is a real risk not so much that the conference may "fail" (i.e., allow the treaty to lapse) as that the Western nuclear possessors may approach the conference in such an apologetic frame of mind that they "give away the store," or at best end up paying for treaty extension several times over. As positions crystalize in the run-up to the conference, it has become clear that the "non-aligned" have four principal concessions that they will seek from the nuclear-weapon states as their price for treaty extension.[1] These are reductions in nuclear arsenals; a CTBT; a cutoff in the production of fissile material for

---

[1]See, for example, the interview with Ambassador Miguel Marin-Bosch of Mexico in *Arms Control Today*, June 1994.

explosive purposes; and a strengthening (perhaps casting in Treaty form) of security assurances, especially those of nonuse. In fact, recent years have seen some striking progress with this agenda. All the recognised NWS excepting China have announced major reductions in their nuclear force plans. All, again excepting China, have ceased nuclear testing; and formal negotiations on a CTBT began in the Conference on Disarmament in Geneva in January 1994. The proposal for a fissile material cutoff is similarly being given a fair wind, with the United Kingdom, initially reluctant to subscribe to the concept, switching to support for it in late 1993.[2] Only on security assurances have the NWS (here excepting China's advocacy of a joint "no first use" declaration) shown little readiness to change their positions.

Nonetheless, anxiety is evident in some quarters as to whether this series of moves will yet be enough.[3] The question arises "enough for what?"--an important question, given the tendency to confuse the declared aim of the "indefinite and unconditional extension"[4] of the Treaty with a realistic negotiating objective for the 1995 conference. Such an aim might be attainable if the issue were decided by a simple majority vote of the signatory states. But it seems widely assumed that this would be politically inadequate: the requirement is seen to be a strong consensus endorsement of the Treaty's extension by the conference.[5] Yet, the reality is that the only thing likely to be

---

[2]In his November 1993 speech at King's College, London, Defence Secretary Rifkind signalled British willingness "to work towards a multilateral regime that will have real nonproliferation benefits." The relative clause should be understood as conditional, not descriptive. But this nonetheless represented a significant shift from earlier British references to lack of stocks of fissile material and willingness merely to keep production to "the minimum necessary."

[3]See, for example, the letter of July 18, 1994, from a coalition of 16 U.S. arms control groups to President Clinton urging the need for a CTBT to be completed as a prior condition for the success of the NPT conference ("Arms Controllers Urge Clinton to Push Nuclear Test Ban," *Defense News*, July 25-31, 1994, p. 21); or the *New York Times* editorial call for new security assurances from the NWS for the same purpose ("Reassuring Non-Nuclear Nations," August 16, 1994, p. A14).

[4]As, for example, in the NATO Summit Declaration of January 11, 1994.

[5]See John Simpson and Darryl Howlett, "The NPT Renewal Conference: Stumbling Toward 1995," *International Security*, Summer 1994.

"enough" to secure indefinite and unconditional extension in this fashion would be a firm commitment by the NWS to the elimination of their arsenals within a near time frame. The "nonaligned" have found that the NPT extension issue has given them powerful leverage over the policies and plans of the NWS; it would be naive to expect them to give up the prospect of such leverage for all time ("indefinite extension") in exchange for anything less than a firm time table for full abolition. Since such a commitment will not be on offer, indefinite and unconditional extension[6] is very likely unattainable--and though it may appropriately remain the banner that members of NATO, the European Union, the G7, and others carry into the negotiation, Western governments will need to remind themselves of this crucial fact in assessing the price that they are prepared to pay for a successful outcome to the conference.

Realism about what is practically attainable should also be combined with realism about the ultimate interests of the NNWS. As noted in Section 4, all NPT adherents share a common interest in the Treaty's continuation. This will not obviate the need for tact and flexibility in the negotiation. Western nuclear possessors must be at pains to show that they have advanced the disarmament agenda. But a clear view of what is attainable at the conference, and of the underlying security interests of the parties, should avoid the need to pay several times over for the best available outcome. Specifically, it should avoid allowing NPT extension to be held hostage to the completion, as opposed to the initiation, of the CTBT and fissile material cutoff agreements. If these arrangements are to be as good as they can be--if they are actually to bite on proliferation and not merely to act as constraints on the recognised NWS--then they must be both verifiable and widely applied. To settle in haste for unsatisfactory regimes[7] simply to meet some perceived deadline associated with the NPT conference would be both to miscalculate what is required to get the best attainable result from the conference and to miss an historic opportunity to tighten nonproliferation restraints.

---

[6]As opposed, for example, to extension by successive fixed periods.
[7]I.e., of limited application and/or lacking in teeth.

Avoiding Reassurance Of Proliferators

Nor should the Western nuclear possessors hurry to strengthen their existing security assurances--a point that relates to the second reason for avoiding an out-and-out Ultimate Evil position on nuclear weapons in extra-European contexts. As argued in Section 4, if their Western possessors go too far in disavowing the relevance of nuclear weapons in non-NATO contexts, they could find they have spurred the very proliferation that they hoped to discourage. The risk is of creating a sort of psychological security vacuum that dependent ally and potential adversary alike might feel drawn to fill.

Advocates of an Ultimate Evil position would retort that their preferred policies, including centrally that of "no first use," still left open the option of countering nuclear force with nuclear force. Indeed, on the lines of the "uniform deterrence" doctrine advocated by Robert Levine,[8] they might argue that the threat of nuclear retaliation against a proliferator's first use could be made if anything *more* compelling if nuclear use in any other circumstance had been abjured. In the discussion in Section 4, we set out some reasons to doubt that this would in practice be the effect. Even, however, if we grant that an Ultimate Evil policy approach would not undermine the West's deterrent effectiveness against new *nuclear* threats, we have to consider other forms of wickedness that might otherwise be amenable in some degree to nuclear deterrence, but which such policies would explicitly exclude from its scope--for example, massive conventional aggression and/or the use of chemical or biological weapons.

As we have discussed, there are severe problems in establishing the credibility of nuclear deterrent threats, explicit or implied, as a counter to any short-of-nuclear aggression in situations where the vital interests of the Western nuclear possessors are not centrally engaged. But that does not mean that the relevance of such threats must be totally excluded--as the nonuse of chemical weapons by Saddam Hussein in the Gulf War arguably demonstrated. Clearly, however, the establishment of nuclear deterrent credibility in such circumstances is made more

---

[8]See Section 2.

difficult by the NWSs' Negative Security Assurances.[9] Not too much weight, it might be argued, should be attached to these. They are self-evidently unenforceable--as we have argued in relation to wider 'no first use' declarations, NSAs could, and no doubt would, be set aside if a particular NWS felt itself sufficiently desperate. Indeed, a potential "target" of nuclear deterrence such as Saddam Hussein would arguably be prone to assume that the NWS would in practice be ready to disregard their own commitments with the same cynicism he would show if the situation were reversed.

All this may be true; but it would be wrong to underestimate the contribution of NSAs to the "self-deterrence" of the NWS--or at least of the democratic ones. The NSAs create a climate of opinion and expectation within which policies and plans are framed; they may not shackle the nuclear possessor, but they represent a significant thread of constraint spun over him. That thread will be strengthened--and be perceived to be strengthened--with each repetition of the assurances, while the workings of the democratic process, with scrutiny by press and opposition parties, will ensure that in a situation of crisis the democratic leader will find himself explicitly challenged to reaffirm them. It will in such circumstances be extraordinarily hard to maintain any degree of ambiguity about whether the adversary (if he is not nuclear-armed) need waste any time at all worrying about the NWS's nuclear option.

But does it really matter if both parties to a confrontation understand that there are no circumstances in which the NWS will resort to nuclear use against the NNWS? There is a growing body of Western analytical opinion that worries about the absence of any perceived counterweight to biological warfare. The 1972 Convention outlawing such weapons contains no provision for verification. Cheap, easy to hide and mass-produce, they have been termed "the poor man's nuclear bomb."[10] As

---

[9]Formal undertakings (first given in 1978) by each of the five recognised NWS not to use their nuclear weapons against NNWS (variously defined and subject to various exceptions).

[10]Graham S. Pearson, "Biological Weapons: The British View," in Brad Roberts, ed., *Biological Weapons: Weapons of the Future?* Washington D.C.: Center for Strategic and International Studies, 1993.

Victor Utgoff has pointed out, "For some types of agents, anthrax for example, a room no larger that a garage can contain a production plant with sufficient capacity to create in a few weeks enough agent to destroy a dozen large cities."[11]

By contrast, the recent trend has been to dismiss the threat of chemical weapons, on the grounds that they require more sophisticated delivery means, need greater quantities of material to achieve a less devastating effect, and are easier to detect and protect against. Yet, what seems a containable risk to the armchair strategist may seem less comfortable to the general in the field who has to confront it. General Norman Schwarzkopf is not known for timidity; but he records the risk of Iraqi use of chemical weapons as his principal dread in preparing the eviction of their armies from Kuwait.[12] Having foresworn retaliation in kind, the Western democracies will be uncomfortably vulnerable to aggression backed with CBW if nuclear deterrence, too, is definitively ruled out.

It is therefore unsurprising if, as suggested by recent press reports (including a preemptive editorial strike by the New York Times[13] against Defense Secretary Perry), the Pentagon's Nuclear Posture Review asked the question whether nuclear threats to deter CBW use should not be "legitimised"--in other words, whether the assurance of nuclear nonuse should not be narrowed to exclude not just nuclear-armed adversaries but those disposing of any form of "weapon of mass

---

[11]Victor A. Utgoff, "The Biotechnology Revolution and Its Potential Military Implications," in Brad Roberts, ed., op. cit.

[12]See H. Norman Schwarzkopf, *It Doesn't Take a Hero*, New York: Bantam Books, 1992, p. 509: "I often reminded my staff: 'You can take the most beat-up army in the world, and if they choose to stand and fight, you're going to take casualties; if they choose to dump chemicals on you, they might even win.' . . . My nightmare was that our units would reach the barriers in the very first hours of the attack, be unable to get through, and then be hit with a chemical barrage. We'd equipped our troops with protective gear and trained them to fight through a chemical attack, but there was always the danger that they'd end up milling around in confusion--or worse, that they'd panic. . . . The possibility of mass casualties from chemical weapons was the main reason we had sixty-three hospitals, two hospital ships, and eighteen thousand beds ready in the war zone."

[13]"Mr. Perry's Backward Nuclear Policy," *New York Times*, March 24, 1994, p. A22.

destruction." What is at issue here, of course, is the right balance between the demands of nonproliferation policy and the requirements of effective deterrence. The former are taken to argue against any dilution of NSAs (indeed, for their strengthening). The latter argue for as much imprecision as possible about the circumstances in which a nuclear-weapon state would be prepared to resort to nuclear use in resisting aggression.

It is not only in the nuclear context that the drawing of clear "lines in the sand" can be a mistake. An aggressive adversary can be counted on to interpret any "thus far and no further" warning as an implicit invitation to come at least thus far. It follows that a threat as dire as that of nuclear use--so hard to credit, even internally, ahead of the shock of the aggression that might justify or demand that form of retaliation--is better left implied than expressly articulated. Indeed, the best sort of threats in international affairs are those that convey a convincing impression that the response to certain forms of extreme behavior will be both dire and ineluctable--but which leave a degree of vagueness about the precise form of that response and do nothing to imply *carte blanche* for any less extreme but still unacceptable conduct.[14] In this manner the would-be deterrer may hope

---

[14]A good example of a skillfully articulated threat of this kind was that reportedly made by James Baker to Tariq Aziz at their January 9, 1991, meeting in Geneva in the run-up to the Gulf War (see Lawrence Freedman and Efraim Karsh, *The Gulf Conflict 1990-1991: Diplomacy and War in the New World Order*, Princeton, New Jersey: Princeton University Press, 1993). "If the conflict starts, God forbid, and chemical or biological weapons are used against our forces, the American people would demand revenge, and we have the means to implement this. This is not a threat, but a pledge that if there is any use of such weapons, our objective would be not only the liberation of Kuwait, but also the toppling of the present regime. Any person who is responsible for the use of these weapons would be held accountable in the future." In this careful utterance, dire ("the toppling of the present regime") and ineluctable ("the American people would demand") consequences are "pledged" if certain extreme behaviour (CBW use) is resorted to--while leaving wholly unclear the means to be used, beyond the ominous observation that they exist. A similar tone was adopted--it remains to be seen whether with similar success--by President Clinton on July 10, 1993 (*Los Angeles Times* of July 11, 1993, p. A1, quoting NBC television) in relation to the possibility of nuclear use by North Korea, when he affirmed that "We would quickly and overwhelmingly retaliate if they

to avoid giving his adversary too clear a view of his options and possibilities, while leaving him scope to "deter himself" by interpreting the threat in accordance with his own worst fears. In short, nuclear deterrence is best served by the avoidance of precision about either the circumstances in which nuclear retaliation should be expected or those in which it could be ruled out.

Clearly, NSAs are inimical to the preservation of such constructive ambiguity. Equally clearly, they are now an established part of the global nonproliferation regime: many of the signatories of the NPT could no doubt fairly claim that without the assurances they would not have acceded to the Treaty. There can, therefore, be no question in foreseeable circumstances of resiling from them--yet, equally, for the reasons set out above, it would seem a disservice to international security if they were to be recast in Treaty form or otherwise strengthened. As former U.K. Defence Secretary Denis Healey memorably expressed it, the first law of holes for those who find themselves in them is to stop digging. If, however, pressure were to grow in the NPT conference end-game, to the point where some movement on NSAs became a political imperative, then the NWS would do well to contemplate acquiescing only in exchange for a narrowing of the scope of the negative assurances so as to exclude chemical- and biological-, as well as nuclear-armed, aggression.

Intellectual Consistency

The third reason to reject the Ultimate Evil concept of nuclear weapons even outside the familiar East-West context of nuclear deterrence is the straightforward intellectual and political difficulty of consistently holding two incompatible views of nuclear weapons, in different contexts but at the same time.

The point is well illustrated by the summary of British Nuclear Policy appearing in the most recent U.K. Defence White Paper.[15] A classic Blessing in Disguise exposition of the role of nuclear weapons

---

were ever to use--to develop and use--nuclear weapons. It would mean the end of their country as they know it."

[15]HMSO, *Statement on the Defence Estimates 1994, Cmnd 2550*, London, April 1994, p. 19.

in Europe nonetheless includes the observation that "Complete and general *nuclear* disarmament [author's emphasis] remains a desirable ultimate goal." The practical problems in the way of a "nuclear free world" are then noted--but not, it seems, the fundamental incoherence in arguing both that nuclear weapons have an indispensable continuing role in European security, and that their abolition would be desirable.

Subscribing to one "law" for Europe and another for the rest of the world is not only intellectually difficult: it also reflects a compartmentalization of the real world that is all too likely to break down over time. Today, it may remain possible to proclaim the security situation in Europe to be *sui generis* and simply to exclude the wider world from U.K. deterrent calculus. Over time, however, events themselves seem likely to blur the Europe/wider-world distinction, if new threats to Europe arise on a North-South as much as an East-West axis. The process of "globalization of security," so well described in the recent French Defense White Paper,[16] must make it increasingly difficult to maintain a concept of European security as something insulated from the rest of the world.

Where then does this leave us? If it is neither politic nor persuasive to advocate a Blessing in Disguise view of nuclear weapons on a global basis--nor yet either politic or prudent to adopt an Ultimate Evil attitude to nuclear weapons outside their traditional East-West context--what position *can* be adopted? There is a simple, if unexciting, answer--to combine a posture of robust defense of the value of nuclear deterrence (that is, the Blessing in Disguise view) in the European context, where it has proved its worth and seems likely to remain an important element of the security equation for at least the foreseeable future, with agnosticism elsewhere.

Agnosticism in this context will mean the avoidance of sweeping claims or broad statements of principle, either touting nuclear deterrence as a universal security panacea, or denying it any efficacy

---

[16]French White Paper on Defense, February 1994, p. 18. See also p. 25 for French acknowledgement of the increasing importance of stability in the Mediterranean and Middle East to France's "strategic interests."

as a force for stability except in the unique circumstances of post-1945 Europe. Agnosticism will mean a refusal to discount the possibility that the sobering shadow of Western nuclear power may induce caution in regional aggressors--just as it will mean a refusal to bank on it. It will mean declining a concept of nuclear weapons in the wider world which would be incompatible with their stabilising role in Europe--while at the same time being pragmatically ready to accept specific initiatives in other parts of the world in the interests of non-proliferation--which would be unacceptable in the European context. And, for the British, it will mean continuing to found the rationale for their nuclear deterrent in European security, while neither claiming nor disclaiming a potential role for it further afield in support of the maintenance of international order.

8. AFTERWORD

WESTERN AND BRITISH NUCLEAR DETERRENCE AFTER THE COLD WAR

With the costs of the Trident deterrent force already substantially incurred, and consensus among the main political parties that Britain should keep nuclear weapons as long as other countries possess them, Britain's retention of a nuclear deterrent until well into the twenty-first century does not seem in doubt. But with what point and purpose? As a lever for encouraging others to give up their own nuclear weapons, or to refrain from acquiring them in the first place--or as a positive contribution to national security, to the collective security of allies and partners in NATO and the European Union, or even to the maintenance of international order in the wider world?

The answer will depend in the first instance on fundamental attitudes to nuclear weapons--attitudes derived as much instinctively as intellectually. Are they good things or bad things? Is the world a safer place with or without them? Are they Blessings in Disguise or an Ultimate Evil?

Ironically, the ending of the Cold War has rendered the case for either proposition more difficult to make with real conviction. As long as the shadow of Soviet power lay across Europe and North America, it could be taken as almost self-evident that only the balance of nuclear terror prevented the outbreak of a third global conflict in the twentieth century. Today, looking back, it is easier to challenge this proposition--to make the argument that East-West confrontation, at least along its central axis through Europe, acquired over time a stability of its own to which nuclear deterrence was largely irrelevant. Or alternatively, even if the war-preventing properties of the nuclear stalemate are conceded, it can be argued that these were to be found only in a specific set of circumstances that no longer exist. The threat of nuclear force, it can also be argued, is only truly credible in the context of a mortal threat to the homeland of the nuclear power or possibly its allies--and of a threat, moreover, fuelled by an ideology so repugnant that the casualties of nuclear action could be viewed as in some sense guilty parties. For the first time in the nuclear age, such conditions no longer obtain--and with their departure/demise, it can be asserted, must go all the old maxims about the value of the nuclear deterrent threat. History has moved on from the sort of major bloc-to-bloc confrontations where nuclear deterrence may once have had some utility; the idea of a war-preventing nuclear threat in a world where the principal security risks stem from terrorism and ethnic conflict is simply outmoded.

Equally, however, a view of nuclear weapons as the Ultimate Evil seems also to have lost plausibility. Arsenals are being reduced, missiles detargeted, hair-trigger postures relaxed; the risks of Armageddon and nuclear winter seem increasingly hard to credit. It is easier now for the supporters of nuclear deterrence to argue that "the Bomb" has in a sense been unfairly stigmatized by its classification as a "weapon of mass destruction." It has long been recognized that many more human lives were lost to the conventional air bombardment of Dresden, or indeed Tokyo, than on the two occasions in the atomic age when nuclear weapons have actually been used. As we near the end of the twentieth century, it can be argued that the label of "weapon of mass destruction" would better fit such more prosaic instruments of slaughter as the assault rifle (which has changed the nature of, for example, tribal warfare in Africa with such appalling consequences), or the land mine (which, by recent estimates,[1] routinely maims and kills more than 1,000 innocents with every month that passes). These, it may be argued, are the true Ultimate Evils of the latter part of the twentieth century; and if nuclear deterrence can play any part in limiting their depredations, then it should not be lightly discarded.

"INSURANCE AGAINST RISKS" VICE "DETERRENCE OF THREATS"

A continuing role for nuclear deterrence, however, is not the same thing as a continuing role for a specifically British nuclear deterrence; and whereas the general rationale may have survived the end of the Cold War, perhaps weakened but still sustainable, the

---

[1] See congressional testimony quoted in "U.S. to Help Raise Money to Find, Defuse Land Mines," *Philadelphia Inquirer*, May 14, 1994, p. 2.

specifically British one clearly has not. The "second center of decisionmaking" concept has lost its saliency. And yet we have argued that neither is there any case for seeking to substitute for it a rationale based primarily on emergent threats beyond the European security context. We have argued that nuclear deterrence may well have a relevance in such new situations, and indeed that an independent U.K. nuclear deterrent might have a contribution to make, in terms of sharing risks and responsibilities as a member of an international "posse"--but we have also argued that neither politics (recalling the requirements of nonproliferation strategy and of London's relations with Washington) nor even reality (recalling the uncertainty of deterrence's applicability in such new contexts and Britain's unreadiness to sign up for global nuclear duties) would allow an extra-European rationale to become the principal foundation upon which the case for the British nuclear deterrent was based. In short, that foundation must remain grounded in the European security situation--and, in the absence of that eyeball-to-eyeball confrontation that lent credibility to the second-center-of-decisionmaking argument, the case for the U.K. deterrent can be expressed only in terms of the cautious preservation in Europe of a security structure that it seems safer to maintain than to dismantle and of substituting for specific deterrence of old threats the more generalized concept of insurance against new risks.

What risks? The answer is perhaps three-fold. The most obvious, as discussed in Section 4, is of a recrudescence, over time, of a threat from the East--now tactfully alluded to as the requirement to "balance" or "take into acount" Russia's weight as Europe's premier military power. This formidable capability, linked with the uncertain political prospects both for Russia's internal development and for her relations with such key neighboring states as Ukraine, is a powerful argument for continuing to give caution priority over optimism in Western defense planning.

Second, the maintenance of nuclear deterrent capabilities may be viewed simply as insurance against the unforeseen. By definition, the risks here are hard to specify in advance of their materialization. But it cannot be ruled out that future threats to European security may emanate from directions quite other than the familiar East-West axis--or even that some new totalitarian threat may emerge in the decades ahead to challenge the Western democracies on a global scale, in a world in which growing interdependence makes any isolationist option increasingly untenable. Such strategic risks may be overlaid with others, born of technological advance. The fact that the NATO allies may feel confident in their current ability to cope by purely conventional means with most forms of aggression other than the nuclear (though also with some hesitancy about biological and chemical warfare) should not be taken as a guarantee that this situation will continue indefinitely. The spectacular rate of scientific innovation, on the contrary, almost ensures that new and more awful weapons will in due course find their way into the armories of aggressive states--weapons to which powerful countersanction would remain essential.

The third risk to be insured against is that the lessons so commandingly taught by the nuclear bomb, that all-out warfare between industrial states in the modern age is no longer a rational pursuit, might come to be forgotten. Those who argue that the integration among European nations achieved within the European Union is already such as to render war impossible would do well to remind themselves that Norman Angell was propounding very much that same theory on the eve of the out-break of the First World War.[2] At some point of human evolution, history may end, and national rivalries may be confined solely to the economic arena--a sort of post-Clausewitzian era in which economic competition becomes the continuation of war by other means. But we are not there yet. Those who would argue that the demonstrated horrors of even nonnuclear war between modern states should be enough to keep the imperative of peace at the forefront of statesmens' minds have to explain why the "war to end wars" was, in the event, no such thing. The prospect of conventional conflict has a perverse fascination that can infect a society--as, again, the First World War demonstrated.[3] No

---

[2]Norman Angell, *The Great Illusion: A Study of the Relation of Military Power to National Advantage*, London: Heineman, 1914.

[3]See Barbara W. Tuchman, *The Guns of August*, New York: Bantam Books, 1976, p. 347 et seq. She illustrates the exalted mood with which many Britons viewed the impending cataclysm with a quotation from Rupert

other antidote to this infection appears as effective as the grimly
unromantic and ineluctable prospect of nuclear destruction.

These, then, are the sort of "insurance against risk" arguments
that can be made for the retention of a British deterrent capability.
Undeniably, they lack the force of the old rationale--not least when it
is recalled that the contribution of the U.K. deterrent will, for the
foreseeable future, be no more than the assumption of a small share of
the risk insurance that will be primarily underwritten by the United
States. Very likely, if Britain today had no nuclear deterrent, the
arguments would not suffice to propel her to acquire one--any more than
they would the Germans, or the Italians. The issue is, however, not
acquisition but retention; and the arguments to justify retaining a
capability that has already been substantially paid for do not have to
be especially powerful when the alternative course of renunciation has
the drawbacks identified in the argument in Section 4.

By this analysis, it should not be especially difficult to sustain
the case for the retention of the U.K. deterrent in the Trident era.
The issue can be expected to stay on the back burner of domestic
politics, and it should not, if adroitly handled, occasion particular
difficulty internationally. Adroit handling will mean accompanying the
retention of the big stick with some very soft speaking. Britain will
have to be at particular pains to emphasize that it sees its deterrent
capability as something essentially at the service of a wider
international community--primarily, but not perhaps exclusively, its
allies and partners in Europe--rather than as an instrument of narrow
national self-interest. It will need to avoid laying claim to any wider
privilege or recognition in consequence of its position as a nuclear-
weapon state. It will have to speak of insurance against risks rather
than deterrence of specific threats; and it will have to underline the
extent to which it has translated the principle of "reduced reliance" on
nuclear weapons into force-plan reductions and relaxation of force
postures. It will have to base its nuclear rationale on the
preservation of a tried-and-tested security structure in Europe, while

---

Brooke's poem "1914"--"To turn, as swimmers into cleanness leaping
Glad from a world grown old and cold and weary. . . ."

combining agnosticism about the utility of nuclear deterrence further afield with strong support for global nonproliferation efforts (to the extent that these do not embody a philosophy of total rejection of nuclear weapons in all security contexts).

THE FUTURE BEYOND TRIDENT?

But perhaps the key question is not so much whether this sort of rationale will be adequate to justify the retention of the U.K.'s nuclear deterrent on the basis of current plans, as whether it will be enough to prevent the demise of the U.K.'s deterrent over a longer time frame by a sort of death-by-atrophy. That same coincidence of the acquisition cycle that makes the bringing-into-service of the Trident force a relatively uncontroversial option also means that the U.K.'s nuclear research and production establishments will shortly find themselves without a central task on which to engage their efforts and skills. The problem will be exacerbated by the continuing inability to conduct nuclear tests. At a time of intense pressure on the defense budget, the nuclear infrastructure must be a particularly tempting target for cuts. Despite a clear commitment of the current government, this sort of consideration must place a question mark against whether the United Kingdom will retain the capability and be able to muster the will, to stay in the nuclear weapon business long-term.

Will Trident be the last British nuclear system? No sensible answer to that question can be attempted at this remove in time. But the argument does at least justify two tentative conclusions. The first is that a more positive vision of the role and purpose of the U.K. deterrent than the rationale sketched above may be needed if the U.K.'s nuclear capability is to be maintained long-term. Inertia, that powerful force in public affairs, currently operates in favor of the retention of capabilities long planned and largely paid for. When it comes to pondering replacements, inertia may pull the other way--and more compelling arguments may then be needed to overcome it. The second conclusion is that, today, the most promising candidate for such a more positive vision is the prospect of the contribution that the British deterrent, teamed with that of France, might one day make to the development of a "common European defense"--perhaps in a world in which closer European integration has been matched by a drifting apart of European and U.S. interests to the point where the U.S. commitment to European security no longer seems as iron-clad as it does today.

Such a new rationale, Eurocentric in terms not merely of geography but also of political identity, may emerge over time to support the continuation of Britain's nuclear role on into the middle and later years of the twenty-first century. Equally, it may not. "Europe" may stumble; or Britain may turn its back on it. Some other rationale, unforeseen here, may emerge--or none may. The optimist may be inclined to view this uncertain prospect in Panglossian spirit. There is justification enough for the present for Britain to maintain her minimum nuclear capability. If the evolution of international security undermines the case for its long-term retention, it will in due course lapse. If, on the other hand, the course of events confirms the desirability of a continuing British nuclear capability, then those events themselves will furnish motive and rationale. Provided no options are prematurely foreclosed, the long-term question may safely be relegated to the verdict of the next century.

APPENDIX A:
BRITAIN, FRANCE, AND THE COSTS OF NUCLEAR INDEPENDENCE

Britain and France, represent different models of nuclear independence--with very different costs attached. Both are committed to the principle that, to be of value, their nuclear deterrents must be fully independent; but each has put its own interpretation on what that independence requires.

For the United Kingdom, operational independence has been enough-- the assured ability of the British prime minister to release the U.K. nuclear deterrent (or, indeed, to withhold it) at any given time, regardless of let or hindrance from any external power. Provided that this minimum operational independence was secure, then the United Kingdom has been content to cooperate with the United States so closely that in many areas vital to the long-term maintenance of the deterrent capability (testing facilities, strategic missile supply, provision of certain materials) any sudden withdrawal of U.S. support could leave the United Kingdom in considerable difficulties. Such an eventuality struck U.K. leaders as so remote as to be not worth the huge costs of ensuring against it by doing everything "in-house."

France took the opposing view. In part, this was a reflection of Gaullist pride; since a large part of the purpose of proceeding with France's nuclear program was to demonstrate France's independence, technological as well as strategic, it would have been self-defeating to seek U.S. assistance. Besides, no such assistance was (initially, at all events) on offer. Accordingly, France set herself the task of doing the whole thing herself, from weapon design to materials acquisition; to warhead development, testing, and production; to delivery system design, production, and integration. The infrastructure requirements were enormous, the technical challenge formidable. The result was a success in which France could justly take pride (even if the achievement may not have been so entirely pure of U.S. assistance as France, and the United States, like to maintain[1]).

There has been, however, a huge bill to pay. France's new defense spending plan for the period 1995 to 2000 allocates 21 percent of the "Title V" equipment monies (Fr613 billion over the six years) to the nuclear deterrent.[2] This, however, represents what the 1994 French Defense White Paper terms "a certain pause in the modernization of our nuclear capability,"[3] and shows a significant decline in the nuclear share, from 33 percent as recently as 1989. Indeed, nuclear preemption of about one-third of the French defense equipment budget was the norm throughout the 1980s.[4] The proportion of the total French defense budget devoted to the deterrent will have been lower ("Title V" usually accounts for about half the overall budget, and the nuclear programs will have made lesser demands on the "operating costs" elements). Nonetheless, it is clear that the "force de dissuasion" (neé "frappe") has absorbed defense funds on a scale commensurate with one of France's three major conventional Armed Forces.

In the United Kingdom, though the figures are cloudy, the outlines of a very significantly lighter burden can be discerned. Answering a parliamentary question in late 1993, a government minister gave figures for "the capital and operating costs associated directly with the strategic deterrent,"[5] over the six years from 1988/1989 to 1993/1994, which represented on average less than 6 percent of the defense budgets for those years. Moreover, those years covered the peak of expenditure on the Trident program. With the total estimated acquisition cost of £11.6 billion (at 1993/1994 prices) averaged over the expected life of the force, and with operating costs estimated at an annual £200 million, this suggests that the United Kingdom is set to obtain 30-years-worth of

---

[1]See, for example, Richard H. Ullman, "The French Connection," *Foreign Policy*, Summer 1989.

[2]"French Plan Bucks Trend in Defence Budgets Cuts," *Jane's Defence Weekly*, May 7, 1994, p. 15.

[3]Op. cit., p. 141.

[4]See Robert S. Norris, Andrew S. Burrows, and Richard W. Fieldhouse, *Nuclear Weapons Databook Volume V*, Boulder, Colorado: Westview Press, 1994, p. 225.

[5]See House of Commons Official Report, October 27, 1993, col. 702.

strategic deterrence for an average annual premium of well under 3 percent of the likely defense budget.[6]

Of course, this is only a part of the story; there are additional costs associated with the maintenance of the Tornado-delivered free-fall nuclear bomb capability, and with the whole nuclear design, production, and maintenance infrastructure (only a portion of which, presumably, are reflected in the published costs of the Trident program). But even if the costs of the strategic deterrent were doubled, or even trebled, to approximate the overall cost of the U.K. nuclear capability, the resource burden is still revealed as strikingly slight compared with that incurred by France's autarkic approach--smaller, in proportional terms, by a factor of two or three.

---

[6]The calculation assumes an average annual capital and operating cost of about £585 million (derived from the figures given above) and a forward U.K. defense budget of some £20.6 billion annually--a figure suggested by Sherard Cowper-Coles ("From Defence to Security: British Defence Policy in Transition," *Survival*, Spring 1994, p. 149) as the likely 1993 value of the cash budget announced by the British government for 1996, the furthest year ahead for which figures are provided.

B: "MININUKES"

Section 5 glanced briefly at the concept of "mininukes"--the idea of a new generation of very low-yield nuclear weapons which, if teamed with the latest precision-guidance technology, might offer a means to strike with "surgical precision" at the key facilities of some future adversary who might not be amenable to traditional nuclear deterrent threats. We noted that the concept was politically stillborn. Nevertheless, it is not without at least academic interest--particularly in view of the criticism it has attracted as not merely inopportune but as wrong *in principle*. British Defence Secretary Rifkind, for example, has condemned the concept in two recent major speeches, arguing that "The implications of such a development of a new warfighting role for nuclear weapons would be seriously damaging to our approach to maintaining stability in the European context. . .,"[1] and that "There is a horror associated with nuclear weapons which we should not attempt to mitigate."[2]

Two separate sorts of objection may be detected here. The point about the "horror" seems to be that if the destructive power of nuclear weapons were too closely assimilated to that of conventional munitions they might lose their "aura of ineluctability" in the eyes of the "deterree." They might, in other words, cease to deter. Conversely, if the present clear firebreak between nuclear and other weapons were reduced, so too might be the powerful inhibitions against their use-- increasing the likelihood that the nearly 50 year record of nonuse would be broken, making further nuclear use on a similar or perhaps larger scale psychologically easier for the future.

It is certainly true that a development process that resulted in the "trivialization" of nuclear weapons would be both dangerous and, ultimately, from the perspective of the nuclear possessor attempting to maintain his deterrent credibility, self-defeating. On the other hand, the concept of the "trivialization" of nuclear weapons seems inherently

---

[1]King's College speech.
[2]Paris speech.

implausible; we may suspect an argument that seems to imply that the
only alternative to so-destructive-as-to-be-unusable is so-reduced-as-
to-be-casually-employed; and we may doubt whether any Western nation
would be prepared to cross even a nuclear firebreak narrowed almost to
the point of invisibility without enormous soul-searching. As with the
housemaid's baby, it would simply not be plausible to seek to brush
aside the first use of nuclear weapons for decades on the basis that "it
was only a little one."

This suggests that considerable further progress could still be
made down the road of making nuclear weapons more precise and
discriminate in their effects, in the interests of making the deterrent
threat of their use more credible, without self-defeatingly depriving
them of their salutary "horror." But what of the second objection noted
above--that such weapons would be for "warfighting" rather than
deterrence? It may help to recall why "warfighting" should be viewed as
objectionable. It is, after all, a nonsense to argue that nuclear, or
any other, weapons should be strictly for deterrence, never use--if they
cannot be used they will not deter. The argument is rather the one that
eventually came to achieve the status of received wisdom in the Cold War
context--that the only rational use for these weapons, if deterrence
failed and war broke out, would be to try to stop it, by inducing the
aggressor to change his mind. This, ultimately political, purpose for
nuclear use stood in sharp distinction from a "warfighting" concept,
which would seek not to stop but to win the conflict through the
specific operational effects of nuclear use on the battlefield—and
which, if practiced between two nuclear-armed adversaries disposing of
virtually unlimited and impregnable nuclear power, would have been an
expressway to mutual annihilation.

Returning to "mininukes," two questions now arise. The first is
why it should be assumed that such weapons would necessarily be "for"
use rather than deterrence. The second is whether it would matter if
they were; in other words, in the fundamentally different situation
where mutual annihilation was no longer a possible consequence of
initiating nuclear use, should not received wisdom's repudiation of
nuclear "warfighting" be up for reconsideration? Part of the answer to

the first question lies in the way in which "mininukes" have been touted as the ideal--perhaps the only--means to attack the command bunkers and the NBC storage and production capabilities of the Third World proliferator. The problem is real enough--there is a demonstrable trend among those whom the Clinton Administration term "backlash states" to seek sanctuary through tunnelling. The "mininuke" sales pitch has therefore tended to concentrate on representing such weapons as "silver bullets" against proliferants, a unique means to dash the weapon from the aggressor's hand.

If this prospect were plausible, we would face a potentially tough dilemma over the second question posed above. Should the Western nuclear possessors fail to avail themselves of such a sovereign specific against a central security challenge of the post-Cold War era, simply in order to uphold a principle? The Rifkind remarks quoted above betray a fear that, if a "warfighting" role for nuclear weapons were accepted in one context, such attitudes could contaminate deterrence closer to home--"be seriously damaging to our approach to maintaining stability in the European context." Is that fair--or would it be tenable to distinguish confrontations of mutual nuclear poossession, where the weapons would continue to be "for deterrence, not use," from confrontations of nuclear monopoly, where the weapons could assume a new disarming role? Yet might not such a distinction also provide a powerful new incentive to proliferation, by suggesting the sort of military utility for a particular class of nuclear weapons that an aggressive despot might find irresistible?

Perhaps fortunately, we need not confront this dilemma--not only because, as noted above, a "mininuke" development program is not on the political cards, but for the more fundamental reason that the whole "silver bullet" concept is invalid. Better means to attack a proliferator's capabilities are certainly required. But the fundamental problem of intelligence--of accurately identifying the myriad dispersal options at the proliferator's disposal--means that the fully effective disarming strike will never be a real-world option. Nor is there compelling reason to believe that mininukes would inevitably be significantly more effective in the role than advanced nonnuclear munitions. And even if there were, common sense suggests that even a half-effective nonnuclear bunker-buster would be more use to the commander in the field than a wholly effective mininuke that he would in all probability be refused political clearance to employ.

In short, there is no case for developing a new generation of more "surgical" nuclear warheads to plug an operational hole that other munitions could not fill. The argument for such development rests solely on the proposition that the chances of nuclear deterrence operating successfully against emergent threats to international security would be enhanced by the availability to Western nuclear-weapon-states of more discriminate nuclear weapons, the use of which could seem more credible in the eyes of the potential "deterree." Such an argument seems neither morally nor logically flawed--merely insufficiently weighty when set against the political case for eschewing new weapon development programs and against the practical argument that available funds would be better spent on developing nonnuclear means to solve the problem of attacking difficult targets.[3]

_____

[3]This, of course, is the path that the U.S. administration has now taken, with then-Defense Secretary Aspin launching a new initiative in a speech to the National Academy of Sciences on December 7, 1993 (see "Pentagon Turns Its Attention to Third-World Arms," *New York Times*, December 8, 1993). *Jane's Defence Weekly* of May 14, 1994 ("Proliferation: the New High Ground for USA," p. 1) reports that "U.S. Deputy Defense Secretary John Deutch is proposing spending $400 milliom a year from FY96 on technology to counter weapons of mass destruction . . . [a] $40 million increase is proposed to develop conventional weapons (lethal and nonlethal) to destroy hardened underground targets."

BIBLIOGRAPHY

Allen, Charles T., "Extended Conventional Deterrence: In from the Cold and Out of the Nuclear Fire?" *The Washington Quarterly*, Summer 1994.

Allison, Graham, Ashton B. Carter, Steven E. Miller, and Philip Zelikow, eds., *Cooperative Denuclearization--from Pledges to Deeds,* Cambridge, Mass.: Center for Science and International Affairs, John F. Kennedy School of Government, Harvard University, 1993.

Angell, Norman, *The Great Illusion: A Study of the Relation of Military Power to National Advantage*, London: Heineman, 1914.

Asmus, Ronald D., Richard L. Kugler, and F. Stephen Larrabee, "Building a New NATO," *Foreign Affairs*, September/October 1993.

Asmus, Ronald D., *Germany in Transition: National Self-Confidence and International Reticence*, Santa Monica, Calif.: RAND, P-7767, 1992.

Aspin, Les, *From Deterrence to Denuking: Dealing with Proliferation in the 1990s,* paper of February 18, 1992.

Booth, Ken, and Nicholas Wheeler, "Beyond Nuclearism," in Regina Cowen Karp, ed., *Security Without Nuclear Weapons?* Oxford: Oxford University Press, 1992.

Bowie, Christopher J., and Alan A. Platt, *British Nuclear Policymaking*, Santa Monica, Calif.: RAND, R-3085-AF, January 1984.

Bundy, McGeorge, George F. Kennan, Robert S. McNamara, and Gerard Smith, "Nuclear Weapons and the Atlantic Alliance," *Foreign Affairs*, Spring 1982.

Bundy, McGeorge, "Nuclear Weapons and the Gulf," *Foreign Affairs*, Fall 1991.

Bundy, McGeorge, William J. Crowe, Jr., and Sidney Drell, "Reducing Nuclear Danger," *Foreign Affairs,* Spring 1993.

Bundy, McGeorge, William J. Crowe, Jr., and Sidney Drell, *Reducing Nuclear Danger: The Road Away from the Brink*, New York: Council on Foreign Relations, 1993.

Campbell, Kurt M., et al., *Soviet Nuclear Fission: Control of the Nuclear Arsenal in a Disintegrating Soviet Union*, Cambridge, Mass.: Center for Science and International Affairs, John F. Kennedy School of Government, Harvard University, 1991.

Carpenter, Ted Galen, "Closing the Nuclear Umbrella," *Foreign Affairs*, March/April 1994.

Carter, Ashton B., William J. Perry, and John D. Steinbruner, *A New Concept of Cooperative Security*, Washington, D.C.: The Brookings Institution, 1992.

President Jimmy Carter, commencement address at Notre Dame University, May 22, 1977.

Clarke, Michael, "British and French Nuclear Forces After the Cold War," *Arms Control*, April 1993.

Cochran, Thomas B., William M. Arkin, and Milton M. Hoenig, *Nuclear Weapons Databook Volume I*, Cambridge, Mass.: Ballinger Publishing Company, 1984.

Cowper-Coles, Sherard, "From Defense to Security: British Defense Policy in Transition," *Survival*, Spring 1994.

Cropsey, Seth, "The Only Credible Deterrent," *Foreign Affairs*, March/April 1994.

Debouzy, Olivier, "A Nuclear Entente Cordiale," *European Brief*, August/September 1993, pp. 50-52.

Debouzy, Olivier, *Anglo-French Nuclear Cooperation: Perspectives and Problems*, London: RUSI, 1991.

Dror, Yehezkel, *Crazy States: A Counterconventional Strategic Problem*, Lexington, Mass.: Heath Lexington Books, 1971.

Dunn, Lewis A., "Rethinking the Nuclear Equation: The United States and the New Nuclear Powers," *The Washington Quarterly*, Winter 1994.

Freedman, Lawrence, *The Evolution of Nuclear Strategy*, New York: St. Martin's Press, 1983.

Freedman, Lawrence, "Britain and Nuclear Weapons," in Michael Clarke and Philip Sabin, eds., *British Defence Choices for the Twenty-First Century*, London and New York: Brassey's, 1993.

Freedman, Lawrence, and Efraim Karsh, *The Gulf Conflict 1990-1991: Diplomacy and War in the New World Order*, Princeton, New Jersey: Princeton University Press, 1993.

Garrity, Patrick J., "The Depreciation of Nuclear Weapons in International Affairs: Possibilities, Limits, Uncertainties," *The Journal of Strategic Studies*, December 1991.

Government of France, *Livre Blanc Sur La Défense*, Paris, February 23, 1994.

Gray, Colin, "Through a Missile Tube Darkly: 'New Thinking' About Nuclear Strategy," *Political Studies*, December 1993.

HMSO, *Statement on the Defence Estimates 1994, Cmnd 2550*, London, April 1994.

Hopkins, John C., and Weixing Hu, eds., *Strategic Views from the Second Tier: The Nuclear Weapons Policies of France, Britain, and China*, San Diego: Institute on Global Conflict and Cooperation, University of California, 1994.

Hosmer, Stephen, *Project AIR FORCE Annual Report,* RAND, AR-3900-AF, 1993.

House of Commons Defence Committee, *The Progress of the Trident Programme, HC 297*, London: HMSO, May 1994.

Joint Communiqué, *Bahamas Meetings, December 1962*, Cmnd. 1915, London: HMSO, 1962.

Joint Declaration by the President of the Russian Federation and the Prime Minister of the United Kingdom of Great Britain and Northern Ireland, Moscow, February 15, 1994.

Kaysen, Carl, Robert S. McNamara, and George W. Rathjens, "Nuclear Weapons After the Cold War," *Foreign Affairs*, Fall 1991.

Kissinger, Henry A., *White House Years*, Boston: Little, Brown and Company, 1979, p. 219.

Legge, J. Michael, *Theater Nuclear Weapons and the NATO Strategy of Flexible Response*, Santa Monica, Calif.: RAND, R-2964-FF, April 1983.

Levine, Robert A., *Uniform Deterrence of Nuclear First Use*, Santa Monica, Calif.: RAND, MR-231-CC, 1993.

Marin-Bosch, Miguel, interviewed in *Arms Control Today*, June 1994.

MccGwire, Michael, "Is There a Future for Nuclear Weapons?" *International Affairs*, Vol. 70, No. 2, 1994.

Mearsheimer, John J., "The Case for a Ukrainian Nuclear Deterrent," *Foreign Affairs,* Summer 1993.

Millot, Marc Dean, "Facing New Nuclear Adversaries," *The Washington Quarterly*, Summer 1994.

Millot, Marc Dean, Roger Molander, and Peter A. Wilson, *"The Day After" Study: Nuclear Proliferation in the Post-Cold War World*, Santa Monica, Calif.: RAND, MR-253-AF (Vol. II, Main Report) and MR-266-AF (Vol. I, Summary Report), 1993.

Ministry of Defence, *The Future United Kingdom Strategic Deterrent Force*, Defence Open Government Document 80/23, London, 1980.

Mitterrand, François, speech at the Palais des Congrès, Paris, January 10, 1992.

Mitterrand, François, speech on Deterrence at the Elysée Palace, Paris, May 5, 1994.

Molander, Roger C., and Peter A. Wilson, *The Nuclear Asymptote: On Containing Nuclear Proliferation*, Santa Monica, Calif.: RAND, MR-214-CC, 1993.

Molander, Roger C., and Peter A. Wilson, "On Dealing with the Prospect of Nuclear Chaos," *The Washington Quarterly*, Summer 1994.

Morgan, Patrick M., *Deterrence: A Conceptual Analysis*, Sage Publications, 1977.

NATO Press Service, *The Alliance's New Strategic Concept*, Brussels, November 7, 1991.

Nitze, Paul H., "Is it Time to Junk Our Nukes? The New World Disorder Makes Them Obsolete," *The Washington Post*, January 15, 1994, p. C1.

———, "Keep Nuclear Insurance," *The Bulletin of the Atomic Scientists*, May 1992.

Norris, Robert S., Andrew S. Burrows, and Richard W. Fieldhouse, *Nuclear Weapons Databook Volume V*, Boulder, Colorado: Westview Press, 1994,

Pearson, Graham S., "Biological Weapons: The British View," in Roberts, Brad, ed., *Biological Weapons: Weapons of the Future?* Washington, D.C.: Center for Strategic and International Studies, 1993.

Perry, William J., "Desert Storm and Deterrence," *Foreign Affairs*, Fall 1991.

Quester, George H., and Victor A. Utgoff, "No-First-Use and Nonproliferation: Redefining Extended Deterrence," *The Washington Quarterly*, Spring 1994.

Quinlan, Michael, "Nuclear Weapons and the Abolition of War," *International Affairs*, Vol. 67, No. 2, 1991.

Quinlan, Michael, "The Future of Nuclear Weapons: Policy for the Western Possessors," *International Affairs*, Vol. 69, No. 3, 1993.

Quinlan, Michael, "British Nuclear Weapons Policy: Past, Present, and Future", in Hopkins, John C., and Weixing Hu, eds., *Strategic Views from the Second Tier: The Nuclear Weapons Policies of France, Britain, and China*, San Diego: Institute on Global Conflict and Cooperation, University of California, 1994.

Rifkind, Malcolm, *"Extending Deterrence?"* speech at a colloquium on strategic issues, Paris, September 30, 1992.

Rifkind, Malcolm, speech at Centre for Defence Studies, King's College, London, November 16, 1993.

Roberts, Brad, ed., *Biological Weapons: Weapons of the Future?* Washington, D.C.: Center for Strategic and International Studies, 1993.

Schwarzkopf, H. Norman, *It Doesn't Take a Hero,* New York: Bantam Books, 1992.

Schelling, Thomas C., *The Strategy of Conflict,* Cambridge, Mass.: Harvard University Press, 1960.

Simpson, John, and Darryl Howlett, "The NPT Renewal Conference: Stumbling toward 1995," *International Security*, Summer 1994.

Tuchman, Barbara W., *The Guns of August*, New York: Bantam Books, 1976.

Ullman, Richard H., "The French Connection," *Foreign Policy*, Summer 1989.

Utgoff, Victor A., "The Biotechnology Revolution and Its Potential Military Implications," in Roberts, Brad, ed., op. cit.

Waltz, Kenneth N., *The Spread of Nuclear Weapons: More May Be Better*, Adelphi Paper No. 171, London: International Institute of Strategic Studies, 1981.

Waltz, Kenneth N., "Nuclear Myths and Political Realities," *American Political Science Review,* September 1990.

Warnke, Paul C., "Missionless Missiles," *The Bulletin of the Atomic Scientists*, May 1992.

Wohlstetter, Albert, "Nuclear Sharing: NATO and the N + 1 Country," *Foreign Affairs,* April 1961.

Wohlstetter, Albert, "Bishops, Statesmen, and Other Strategists On the Bombing of Innocents," *Commentary*, June 1983.

Yost, David S., *Western Europe and Nuclear Weapons,* Livermore, California: Center for Security and Technology Studies, Lawrence Livermore National Laboratory, University of California, 1993.

Yost, David S., "France and the Gulf War of 1990-1991: Political-Military Lessons Learned," *The Journal of Strategic Studies*, September 1993.

Yost, David S., "Nuclear Weapons Issues in France," in Hopkins, John C., and Weixing Hu, eds., *Strategic Views from the Second Tier: The Nuclear Weapons Policies of France, Britain and China*, San Diego: Institute on Global Conflict and Cooperation, University of California, 1994.

MR-514-AF

ISBN 0-8330-1619-9

50900

9 780833 016195

MR-514-AF